GOD
FIRST

FOR A BETTER LIFE

BIBLICAL PRINCIPLES FOR BETTER LIVING

COLVIN BLANFORD, REL.D.

EQUIP
P R E S S

Copyright © 2021 Colvin Blanford

All rights reserved. No part of this publication may be reproduced, distributed, or transmitted in any form or by any means, without prior written permission.

Published by Equip Press, Colorado Springs, CO

Scripture quotations marked (NIV) are taken from the Holy Bible, New International Version. Copyright © 1973, 1978, 1984, 2011 by Biblica, Inc.® Used by permission. All rights reserved worldwide.

Scripture quotations marked (NRSV) are taken from the New Revised Standard Version Bible, copyright © 1989 the Division of Christian Education of the National Council of the Churches of Christ in the United States of America. Used by permission. All rights reserved.

First Edition: 2021
God First / Colvin Blanford
Paperback ISBN: 978-1-951304-54-6
eBook ISBN: 978-1-951304-55-3
Library of Congress Control Number: 2021902336

ACKNOWLEDGMENTS

After acknowledging Jesus Christ as my Lord and Savior, it was a blessing to be baptized on Easter Sunday morning 1945, at 5 a.m., at the Olive Grove Baptist Church in Kemp, Texas. It was a blessing to continue my spiritual nurture and growth at Bethlehem Baptist Church in Terrell, Texas, and at historic Third Baptist Church in San Francisco.

I am grateful to all of my relatives, friends and colleagues who have touched and have had an impact on my life.

I am grateful to have had the opportunity and privilege to serve as pastor of First Baptist Church, Gary, Indiana and to have had the honor and privilege of being the organizing pastor of Cosmopolitan Baptist Church in San Francisco, California; Christ Baptist Church, Gary, Indiana; Christ Baptist Church, Chicago, Illinois; and New Life Christian Fellowships International, Mesa, Arizona.

It has also been an honor and privilege to serve as adjunct professor, affiliate professor, associate professor teaching in the areas of Black church studies, preaching, and social ethics, as director of Black church studies and as a member of the Board of Trustees at Northern Seminary.

DEDICATION

This book of sermons is dedicated to my devoted wife, Margaret Ann Blanford and to my deceased parents, John Hardee Blanford (1907–1980) and Hattie Ellen Blanford (1908–1993).

PREFACE

In August 2018, I was blessed to preach at Christ Baptist Church in Gary. After the services, we were being greeted by our many friends and former members. One of them asked me how I was doing and I told her: "I'm blessed and highly favored!"

She proceeded to tell me that in the Bible only Mary was referred to as being "highly favored." I graciously acknowledge that the angel did tell Mary that she had been highly favored. And proceeded to say to her: "I cannot speak for anyone else, but I know beyond the shadow of any doubt that I have not only been blessed by the Lord but I have also been highly favored."

I have been blessed with salvation. I have been blessed to have the privilege to preach and teach the gospel and to help make disciples for Jesus Christ. I have been blessed to plant churches. I was blessed to be mentored by my pastor, the late Dr. F.D. Haynes, Sr. and to have had the privilege and opportunity to mentor other pastors.

I have been blessed with a loving wife and with a loving family and with many devoted friends and colleagues. I have been blessed in more ways that I can possibly mention.

But I have also been highly favored.

In September 1976, I was told that I had six to eighteen months to live and that if I had surgery there was a 50-50 chance that I would not survive. I was told that if I did survive, I could possibly live the rest of my live in a vegetative state.

So surgery was not an option. I thanked God for the time he had given me and for whatever time I would have.

My wife, Margaret, went to the Lord in prayer. She told the Lord that our two sons needed a father to raise them. So she asked the Lord to take her and leave me to raise our two sons.

The next month, when I went to the hospital for my check up, some more x-rays were taken. When my doctor looked at them, he had a strange look on his face. He said to me: "Pastor, (and I was his pastor) look at this." I looked and had no idea what I was looking at or what the x-rays meant. Then he placed the x-rays that were taken the previous month beside these x-rays. Immediately, I noticed that the lines that were on the first set of x-rays were not on the one's just taken. MIRACULOUSLY, the lines that were there the month before were gone and "my death sentence" had been lifted!

As I look back on that experience (and other experiences) I realize that I have not just been blessed by the Lord but I have also been "HIGHLY FAVORED!"

One Friday night in the summer of 1954, I was watching The Friday Night Fights. During a commercial, I went to the kitchen to get some refreshments. As I stood at the kitchen sink, all of a sudden, I felt this overwhelming sensation that God was calling me to preach. I was stunned and terrified. As this indescribable sensation overwhelmed me, I began to cry uncontrollably and I cried out: "No, Lord! Not that! I'll do anything you want me to do. But, not that."

During the next two years, I "ran" from that calling. I didn't mind serving the Lord in some way, but I definitely didn't want to preach. But the call did not go away.

Several months before graduating from high school in June 1956, I got fed up with this feeling that God was calling me to preach. So I decided to challenge God. One day, I got so fed up that I told God: "If you really want me to preach, give me a title and text."

I said this defiantly and immediately became terrified because I had insulted God. For a period of time, God was silent and I was scared.

PREFACE

After a while, a verse of scripture kept running through my mind several times a day. I'd be trying to think about or do something else and that verse kept being repeated in my mind over and over again. That verse was: *"I am not ashamed of the gospel for it is the power of God unto salvation to everyone who believes. To the Jew first and also to the Greek."*

I had no idea where to find that scripture, so I ask my pastor, Dr. F. D. Hayes, Sr. He told me that it was in Romans 1:16. Then the title came to me: "There's Power in God's Word."

Pastor Haynes scheduled me to preach my first sermon at the evening service on Father's Day 1956. My text was Romans 1:16. My sermon title was "There's Power in God's Word."

Since that time, I have been blessed to preach (or at least, try to preach) some five thousand sermons. After a lot of prodding from Dr. J. Alfred Smith Sr. I submitted a manuscript for the book he was editing in 1976 on Outstanding Black Sermons. The manuscript was accepted and the sermon was published.

Over the years, people have asked me about publishing some of my sermons. I didn't think seriously about doing so until fairly recently. After much prayer, I believe the Lord is leading me to do so at this time.

As I was preparing to undertake this project, I was reminded of something that Dr. Caesar Clark said many years ago. He was preaching a city-wide revival at the Oakland auditorium in Oakland, California. Each night people were praising him for the sermon he preached. One night he told them: **"No man has it all. God has given to each man just a portion."**

Indeed, God has given to each man and woman just a portion. I thank God for the portion He has given me and for the privilege of sharing a portion of that portion with others.

This project is a response to some of the most prevalent personal, family and social issues that people face today and will address themes such as: Biblical Principles for Better Living; Dealing with Difficult

Things; Help for the Christian Home; Don't Give Up!, and What Do These Stones Mean?

Every Sunday, millions of people throughout the country and around the world take the opportunity to hear God's Word. Some of them hear God's Word on the radio or on the television. Some of them travel long distances to the place where someone gives them a message based upon God's Word. Some of them don't miss a Sunday. Some of them attest to not missing a single Sunday in several years.

All of this is well and good, but there's a problem. The problem is: **most people who hear God's Word on a regular basis are not living by it.**

When I was pastoring First Baptist Church in Gary, there was a sign in the junior high classroom that read:

"If you were arrested for being a Christian
Would there be enough evidence to convict you?"

Based upon what the Bible teaches us about being a Christian and living the Christian life, if most of people who profess to be a Christian were arrested there certainly would not be enough evidence to convict them.

By their actions, and often by their own admission, most people who profess to be a Christian don't take God's Word very seriously.

Why? Obviously, there are many factors involved. Many sermons have been preached on these "factors" but few sermons pay close attention to the basic reason behind these "factors."

After all is said and done, the basic and fundamental reason why most people who hear God's Word on a regular basis give evidence of not taking it very seriously is because **God's Word has not really penetrated their lives**.

In the parable of the sower, the seed and the soil found in Matthew 13:1-9, Jesus tells us that whether a crop is productive depends on the condition of the soil.

PREFACE

It is clear from this parable that whether a seed produces a crop is not determined by where the seed is sown but on the condition of the soil.

Regardless of the ability of the sower and regardless of the truth of the seed, the seed has to penetrate the soil in order to have a chance of producing a crop. Seed that does not penetrate the soil can never produce a crop.

Unfortunately, most people who hear the Word of God never produce a crop because that Word never penetrates their lives. It remains on the surface. It never gets inside of them where it can germinate and produce a crop.

It is imperative that Biblical principles penetrate our lives and germinate in order for us to live the lives that God wants us to live and produce the crop that He wants us to product.

Most people don't realize that regardless of the influence of the sower (the preacher/teacher) and regardless of the truth of the seed (God's Word), God's Word will not have the desired effect on their lives if the "soil" (the person) is not willing to accept, internalize, and live by God's Word.

In light of this observation, this book of sermons is being presented in the hope that the Holy Spirit will use it to help more people to move from where they are to where they need to be in order to glorify God, to edify His Church, and to advance His Kingdom.

Colvin Blanford, Rel.D.
God First = Better Life

FOREWORD

We owe a tremendous debt of gratitude to my friend, Dr. Colvin Blanford, for writing a powerfully gripping and relevant book of impactful sermons—sermons that scratch where we itch, to use Edgar Jackson's term. These sermons speak with freshness to the issues of our day—issues such as family needs, disappointments and difficulties, racism, how to live a more spiritually fruitful life, the need to have a clearer and more healthy appreciation for our African American heritage, and perspectives on how to improve our criminal justice, educational, economic, and political systems.

A careful reading of these sermons/messages will help one to see that out of his background of deep spirituality and astute scholarship that Dr. Blanford has ferreted out some biblically based, doctrinally-sound and life-centered sermonic messages. They can serve as models for modern preaching content and style.

For the pastor/teacher who finds merit in series preaching, Dr. Blanford's book of sermons can also serve as a model in how to arrange attractively a series of sermons.

Another factor that makes these sermons attractive and meaningful is the fact that our author has been blessed with such a wide variety of experiences; having preached for more than sixty (60) years, pastored for more than fifty (50) years, worked in corporate America for a stint, and served simultaneously during part of those years as an associate and adjunct professor at Northern Baptist Theological Seminary in Lombard, Illinois (1974-1991).

I have had the joy of hearing my friend, Colvin, preach on many occasions in various venues, and each time his sermons were filled with solid content, sincere passion, and laced with tasteful humor. They are also characteristically clear and cogent.

I tend to agree with Dr. Martin Luther King, Jr. that sermons are not basically intended to be read but to be heard. They are more for the ear than for the eye. However, I thank God for the time and labor that persons have given to craft sermons in written form. And so, I thank Dr. Colvin Blanford for having labored long and sacrificially to leave a powerful legacy of sermonic nuggets for this generation and generations to come.

— **Julius R. Scruggs,** *Pastor-Emeritus*
First Missionary Baptist Church
Huntsville, Alabama

ENDORSEMENTS

I have known Dr. Blanford since the early seventies. He has been a great friend, good counselor and mentor in my development as a pastor …. He has ministered to our church on many occasions and he is still actively serving the Lord in his golden years of retirement. Dr. Blanford has demonstrated his commitment to the local church, church planting and the training and developing of young pastors.

His faithfulness to this task leaves a great legacy for Christian leaders who will follow him. I was impressed by the variety of topics that he chose to cover in this book and his willingness to address our social and political systems. We have much food for thought from his scholarship.

I recommend this book as a valuable treasure for one's theological library and good reading material for anyone who wants to grow in their ministry and finish well.

— **Lucious Fullwood,** *M.Div., D. Min.*
Bellevue Baptist Church
Chicago, Illinois

I am grateful and privileged to have had, and still have, a personal relationship with Dr. Colvin Blanford, with the irony of it being that he chose me. Dr. Blanford is that kind of preacher/pastor—he

GOD FIRST

makes himself available to younger pastors that he might pour into them the richness of God's Word, and as a mentor, guide them to fulfilling, with humility, the plan that God has for their life Dr. Blanford shows himself as a modern-day Paul, one who is convinced about the power of God's Word, convinced when it comes to witnessing about the power of God's Word, and confident in his standing on the power of God's Word.... Dr. Blanford's preaching and teaching have always been well received as well as a blessing....

— **Chet Johnson,** *Sr., Pastor*
New Tabernacle Baptist Church
Gary, Indiana

I was and I remain filled with excitement and expectation of the wealth of knowledge I and many others, both preachers and layperson, will receive as we dig into the field of diamonds ... in this inspired work... I want to shout to the nation of people seeking for the first time or seeking God for a way to make living life better, "Help in on the way," in the form of a book entitled, "God First for a Better Life" by Colvin Blanford.

— **Queen Esther Thomas,** *Minister*
Gary, Indiana

It is a privilege to be able to read the introduction and synopsis of Rev. Blanford's upcoming book... I have also been privileged to listen to some of these messages in person and I can testify

ENDORSEMENTS

to the impact they have had on my life personally and the life of my family collectively. This book is packed with real world applicable examples that are needed by today's Christian in order to be equipped for the day-to-day challenges of Christlike living. Pastor Blanford explores every aspect of human living in this book, helping individuals deal with personal issues, as well as deal with issues in the home and in the community at large. This is a must read for every believer.

— **Aisosa Ayela-Uwangue**
Chandler, Arizona

Through this book of sermons, Colvin Blanford reminds us that the Word of God is relevant for all times, especially for the 21st Century. These sermons speak to the different ages and stages of life.

By including in this book of sermons his commentary that focus on current social systems of injustice as well as a preliminary plan of action for the reader's reflection, Colvin Blanford sends a clarion call to us Christians. We Christians, in addition to being concerned about the spiritual well-being of ourselves and others, must individually and corporately as the Church of Jesus Christ, be concerned about and address those systems of injustice that hinder people and groups of people from experiencing their God-given potential.

— **Michelle Cobb,** *Pastor and former*
Conference Superintendent
Indiana Conference of the United Methodist Church

As a five-fold ministry gift of the body of Christ, I have had the privilege of being discipled and mentored by Dr. Colvin Blanford. And I am honored to say that his influence and discipleship are still prevalent in my life today. As you read the anointed pages of this Holy Spirit inspired message, allow the words of God to move past the surface level and penetrate your life so that you can experience the abundant life that God has in store for you.

— **Annette Walker,**
author of The Destiny Point Experience

As enlightened as I found myself after reading your journey to Jesus Christ, I was very impressed by your choice of sermons.

— **Alfred Carfora**
Gilbert, Arizona

We relocated from Ft. Wayne, Indiana to Tempe, Arizona, so we have only known Rev. Blanford for two years. We were led to join New Life Christian Fellowships Church in Mesa, AZ. This afforded us the opportunity to hear Rev. Blanford's sermons on numerous occasions… After reading his book, it brought his sermons to life. We enjoyed an in-depth understanding of God's Word. Rev. Blanford is a true man of God, and this is exemplified in his informative, spirit-filled, and effervescent sermons. "A wonderful book."

— **Robert & Ann Nichols**
Tempe, Arizona

ENDORSEMENTS

Dr. Blanford: Thank you for allowing me to view this wonderful work. You, sir, have been more than blessed, you have been a blessing. Your admonitions to study, to rightly divide the word of truth, and to live by faith, have guided my ministry like the North Star. May this book of sermons do the same for those who have an ear to hear.

— Dwight A. Gardner
Trinity Baptist Church
Gary, Indiana

Dr. Colvin Blanford provides powerful, personal and pertinent principles on living not only a better life, but the best life. He gives Godly advice on every aspect of daily living for persons at various seasons and situations in life. This book's contents affirms that the God who made us continues to guide us.

—Warren H. Stewart, Sr.
First Institutional Baptist Church
Phoenix, Arizona

CONTENTS

Acknowledgments	5
Dedication	7
Preface	9
Foreword	15
Endorsements	17

1. BIBLICAL PRINCIPLES FOR BETTER LIVING	33
Needed: A Spiritual Overhaul	**33**
Advantage of Disadvantages	40
Essentials for Spiritual Growth	46
Getting Rid of Excess Baggage	52
Good Advice from God's Word	58
From Hard Times to Hallelujah	65

2. DEALING WITH DIFFICULT THINGS	73
Dealing with Doubt	73
Dealing with Disappointment	79
Dealing with Disaster	85
Dealing with Death	91

3. HELP FOR THE CHRISTIAN HOME	97
Help for Christian Couples	97
Help for Christian Parents	106
Help for Christian Children	112
Help for Christian Mothers	117
Help for Christian Fathers	123
Building Your Home on a Strong Foundation	129
From the Pig Pen to the Father's House	135

4. DON'T GIVE UP	141
Don't Give Up on God	141
Don't Give Up on Your Marriage	150
Don't Give Up on Your Children	158
Don't Give Up on Yourself	166

5. WHAT DO THESE STONES MEAN?   173
    What Do These Stones Mean?   173
    What Do These Stones Mean?   181
    What Do These Stones Mean?   191
    What Do These Stones Mean?   198

6. GOING TO THE NEXT LEVEL   203
    Responses to Racism   203
    Repentance That Leads to Social Justice & Racial Reconciliation   210
    What Racial Reconciliation Looks Like   218
    God First for a Better Life   233

7. OBSERVATIONS FOR REFLECTION & ACTION   241
    Fixing our Criminal Justice System   241
    Fixing our Educational System   259
    Fixing our Economic System   266
    Fixing our Political System   271

CHAPTER ONE
"Principles for Better Living"

Chapter one will focus on the theme "Principles for Better Living" The topics for these sermons are:

"Needed: A Spiritual Overhaul"
"Advantages of Disadvantages"
"Essentials for Spiritual Growth"
"Getting Rid of Excess Baggage"
"Good Advice from God's Word"
"From Hard Times to Hallelujah"

These topics are important because they address spiritual issues that people face and offer biblical insights for responding to them.

The first sermon in this chapter, "Needed: A Spiritual Overhaul," is based on Psalm 51:10 and will look at the need for a spiritual tune up, power steering, power brakes and taking down your rear-view mirror. Doing these things can facilitate spiritual growth.

The second sermon, "Advantages of Disadvantages," is based on 2 Corinthians 12:1-10 and will focus on why some negative things can have positive results in our lives. This sermon can help to affirm the fact that "All things work together for good for those who love the Lord and are called according to His purpose."

"Essentials for Spiritual Growth" is based on 2 Peter 1:3-9 and will focus on the need for spiritual goodness, knowledge, self-control and perseverance. This sermon will seek to make a case for these virtues being essential for spiritual growth.

"Getting Rid of Excess Baggage" is based on 1 Peter 2:1-3 and will deal with the importance of getting rid of the spiritual baggage of malice, deceit and hypocrisy. Many people don't realize that holding on to these

25

things do themselves great harm. The sermon will encourage people to ask the Lord to help them to get rid of them.

"Good Advice from God's Word" will focus on the advice given in Proverbs 3:5-6 by looking at The Principle ("Trust in the Lord with all thine heart") and by looking at The Promise ("In all thy ways acknowledge Him and He shall direct thy paths").

Many people try to do things on their own before turning to the Lord for help. This sermon will encourage them to seek the Lord first and do what He tells them to do.

"From Hard Times to Hallelujah" is based on 2 Kings 7:1-11 and encourages us to hold on to our faith and trust God to show us what to do to turn things around when things seem to not be going our way.

CHAPTER TWO
"Dealing with Difficult Things"

Chapter two will focus on "Dealing with Difficult Things." The topics for these sermons are:

"Dealing with Doubt"
"Dealing with Disappointment"
"Dealing with Disaster"
"Dealing with Death"

The first sermon in this chapter "Dealing with Doubt" is based on Mark 9:14-24 where Jesus heals a father's son who had been possessed by a demon that robbed him of his speech and made him suicidal.

The second sermon, "Dealing with Disappointment," is based on Luke 5:1-11, where Simon Peter and his companions had been fishing all night without catching any fish. When Jesus advised them to "launch out into the deep," they were astonished at the great number of fish that they caught.

The next sermon in this chapter, "Dealing with Disaster," is based on Job 1:13-21, where Job had to deal with the loss of his property, the loss of his health, and the death of his seven sons and three daughters.

The final sermon in this chapter, "Dealing with Death," is based upon John 11:1:1-6 and 17:21, where Mary and Martha had to deal with the death of their brother, Lazarus.

CHAPTER THREE
"Help for The Christian Home"

Because the home has been under attack since the Garden of Eden, chapter three has seven sermons to help families: couples, parents, and children. The topics covered are:

"Help for Christian Couples"
"Help for Christian Parents"
"Help for Christian Children"
"Help for Christian Mothers"
"Help for Christian Fathers"
"Building Your Home on a Strong Foundation"
"From the Pig Pen to the Father's House"

"Help for Christian Couples" will look at some misconceptions of Ephesians 5:22-33 and attempt to put them in proper perspective. In doing so, we will affirm the Biblical perspective that, although the husband is the head of the family, the husband and wife are mutually accountable to each other.

"Help for Christian Parents" will look at Proverbs 22:6 and will point out that the way a child "should go" is to live by the principles of God's Word.

"Help for Christian Children" will focus on Ephesians 6:1-3. We will point out that parents are responsible to teach their children to live according to God's Word. We will point out that children are not obligated to "obey" their parents if they are told to do something illegal or ungodly. We will also affirm that children are to "honor" (respect) their parents whether their parents teach them to do right or to do wrong.

"Help for Christian Mothers" will look at lessons mothers can learn from the Canaanite woman in Matthew 15:21-28. This mother knew that her daughter had a problem. This mother saw her daughter's problem as her problem, too. This mother got help for her daughter.

"Help for Christian Fathers" is based on Ephesians 6:4 and will look at how fathers can exasperate their children and at how fathers can bring up their children in the discipline and instruction of the Lord.

"Building Your Home on a Strong Foundation" is based on Deuteronomy 6:4-9 and will look at what we can learn from the *Shema* about building our home on a strong biblical foundation. Husbands and wives will be encouraged to build their lives on God's Word by reading, studying, and meditating on it daily and by displaying verses from the Word of God in and around the home so they and their children will have constant reminders of God's Word, God's will, and God's promises.

"From the Pig Pen to the Father's House" is based on Luke 15.11-24. The prodigal son started out asking his father to "give me" his share of the estate and ended up with him asking his father to "make me" a hired servant. Between these two statements, the Prodigal Son was in the pig pen. We will look at what the "pig pen" may symbolize for us and what we need to do to go "from the pig pen to the Father's house."

CHAPTER FOUR
"Don't Give Up!"

Because there are times when each of us is overwhelmed by some of the challenges of life, sometimes we feel like giving up. Therefore, this chapter will focus on four pertinent topics:

"Don't Give Up on God"
"Don't Give Up on Your Marriage"
"Don't Give Up on Your Children"
"Don't Give Up on Yourself"

"Don't Give Up on God" is based on Genesis 32:22-28, where Jacob and Esau, as they faced their challenging personal issues, didn't give up on God. Because of the many challenges of life, there are times when people feel like giving up on God, and sometimes actually do, give up on God. This sermon will encourage them to not give up on the One who has the unlimited power and resources to help them.

"Don't Give Up on Your Marriage" is based on Matthew 19:1-6. With the divorce rate continuing to escalate, couples need to be encouraged to not give up on their marriage. Jesus speaks to this issue in Matthew 19:1-6 and tells us what we should do and why we should do it.

"Don't Give Up on Your Children" is based on the experience of the Canaanite woman in Matthew 15:21-28. Parenting can be frustrating. Sometimes parents want to give up. Sometimes parents are ready and willing to throw up their hands and "throw in the towel." In this sermon, parents are encouraged to consider what this mother did. Rather than "giving up" on her child, she "gave" her child "over" to a Higher Power. Reference will be made to Monica, the mother of Augustine, who refused to give up on her wayward son. As a result, he came to Christ, became a

Christian and a priest, and eventually became one of the great "fathers" of the early church.

The last sermon in this series, "Don't Give Up on Yourself," is based on Psalm 51:1-10 and encourages people to not give up on themselves because of their sins and shortcomings but to follow the example of King David by repenting and asking for Divine help.

CHAPTER FIVE
"What Do These Stones Mean?"

There are four sermons on the topic "What Do These Stones Mean?" in this chapter. Each of the four sermons is based on the question that the children of Israel were encouraged to be able to answer in light of the stones of memorial that had been placed in the Jordan River.

The stones that we will be dealing with in this chapter are significant "stones" in the African-American experience. It is important that not only African-Americans, but that people of other cultures and ethnic groups understand and appreciate, the resilience of Black Americans of African descent.

"What Do These Stones Mean? is based on Joshua 4:1-7 and consists of four sermons addressing five different "stones" from the African-American experience: The Heritage Stone. Two Mill Stones. Stones of Protest. Stepping Stones and the influence of The Eternal Stone: "The Stone that the builders rejected."

CHAPTER SIX
Going to The Next Level

This chapter has four sermons that focus on repentance that leads to social justice and racial reconciliation. In the first sermon, "Responses to Racism," I will reflect on some of my personal experiences as an African-American, look at the response of Jesus to the Samaritan woman and at the response of Daryl Davis to the Ku Klux Klan. The next two sermons focus on "Repentance That Leads to Social Justice & Racial Reconciliation" and on "What Racial Reconciliation Looks Like." The last sermon will take us back to our basic premise of putting GOD FIRST FOR A BETTER LIFE.

CHAPTER SEVEN
Observations for Reflection & Action

The last chapter will offer some personal observations for "fixing" our broken social systems. Obviously, none of these observations can "fix" any of these problems but will simply look at some possible actions that can be part of a more thorough and comprehensive plan. In that sense, this final chapter will offer observations on Fixing Our Criminal Justice System, Fixing Our Educational System, Fixing Our Economic System, Fixing Our Political System and will encourage readers to reflect upon them and take action as they are led, guided, directed, and empowered by the Holy Spirit.

CHAPTER ONE

BIBLICAL PRINCIPLES FOR BETTER LIVING

"Needed: A Spiritual Overhaul"
"Advantages of Disadvantages"
"Essentials for Christian Growth"
"Getting Rid of Excess Baggage"
"Good Advice from God's Word"
"From Hard Times to Hallelujah"

NEEDED: A SPIRITUAL OVERHAUL
Psalm 51:10 (KJV)

INTRODUCTION

Most car manufacturers suggest that you take your car in for a maintenance checkup about every 3,000 miles. These checkups usually include changing the oil and filter. Sometimes a complete checkup or tune-up is needed. Sometimes the tires need to be rotated and other work performed.

When it comes to our spiritual nurture. When it comes to our spiritual growth and development, there is some spiritual maintenance that needs to take place. Sometimes, a complete spiritual overhaul is needed.

OBSERVATION

In Psalm 51, King David acknowledges his spiritual weaknesses. He acknowledges his sins and shortcomings and that he is in need of a complete spiritual overhaul. He makes this clear in verse 10 when he asks the Lord to: *"Create in me a clean heart, O God, and renew a right spirit within me." (Ps. 51:10, KJV)*

Every now and then, we need a spiritual check-up. Every now and then, we need to evaluate our spiritual health. Every now and then, we need to take a complete inventory of our spiritual growth and development. When we do this honestly, we will discover that we are in need of a spiritual overhaul.

Based upon this observation, two basic questions need to be raised and answered.

The First Question: What is the Problem?

The first question that needs to be raised and answered is: "What is the problem?" What is the basic and fundamental problem that we face? What is the basic and fundamental problem that plagues us?

Although the answer to that question is simple the answer is quite significant. The basic and fundamental human problem we have to face and deal with is the spiritual problem of SIN.

Behind every human problem that we face in our society and behind every human problem in the whole world is the problem of sin.

When people talk about the drug problem, they are really talking about the problem of sin. Sin—missing the mark, disobeying God, placing our desires and our will above the will of God, being more concerned about the temporary than about the eternal—is at the heart of the drug problem.

Sin is at the heart of every relationship problem. Sin is at the heart of every problem in society. Sin is at the heart of racism. Sin is at the heart of sexism. Sin is at the heart of discrimination. Sin is at the heart

BIBLICAL PRINCIPLES FOR BETTER LIVING

of prejudice. Sin is at the heart of injustice. Sin is at the heart of double standards. Sin is at the heart of greed. Sin is at the heart of hypocrisy. You name it, sin is at the heart of it.

A few years ago, I came across a statement that described sin as: "SPIRITUAL INFLUENCE NONEXISTENT."

When we refuse to be influenced by God's will as found in God's Word and be influenced by God's purpose for our lives, we are guilty of sin.

It is also true that we sin when we allow other things to influence us more than God's Word.

For many years now, I have spelled sIn. Why? Because "I" is at the heart of sin. Self and selfishness are at the heart of sin. Therefore, the basic and fundamental problem that each of us has to deal with in life is the problem of sin.

Sin will continue to be our basic and fundamental problem until we are willing to say to the Lord:

"NOT MY WILL, BUT THINE BE DONE!"
The Second Question:
What do we need to do about the problem?

Since sin is our basic and fundamental problem, what do we need to do about this problem? What do we need to do about the problem of sin?

I believe that we all need to start by doing what David did in Psalm 51:10. In this verse, after acknowledging his sins and shortcomings, King David asked the Lord to *"Create in me a clean heart and renew the right spirit within me."*

Basically, the heart is the person. The heart is the core of one's being. Biblically, your heart is you. That's why the Scripture says, "As a man thinks in his heart so is he."

To ask for a clean heart is to ask God to cleanse you of all sin and

35

unrighteousness. To ask for a clean heart is to ask God to make you a new person in Jesus Christ. To ask for a clean heart is to ask God to give you a spiritual overhaul.

To have "the right spirit" is to have "the right attitude." Your attitude reflects your spirit. Your spirit reflects your attitude.

That means: If you have a mean attitude it's because you have a mean spirit. If you have a pleasant attitude it's because you have a pleasant spirit. If you have an unpleasant attitude it's because (at least at that moment) you have an unpleasant spirit. If you have a godly attitude it's because you have a godly spirit. If you have an ungodly attitude it's because (at least at that moment) you have an ungodly spirit. Why? Because your attitude reflects your spirit.

Because we're imperfect human beings, there are times when all of us need a spiritual overhaul.

SOME OF US NEED A NEW ENGINE

A new engine is a new heart. That's why there are times when all of us need to ask the Lord to create in me a clean heart and renew the right spirit within me.

SOME OF US NEED NEW SPARK PLUGS

Some of us need new spark plugs because we have lost our spiritual power. Some of us have lost our spiritual zeal. Some of us have lost our spiritual fervor.

SOME OF US NEED POWER STEERING

Some of us have stopped asking and letting the Lord "steer" our lives. Some of us have stopped asking and letting the Lord lead, guide, direct and empower our lives. In order to regain that power steering, we need to trust in the Lord with all of our heart. We need to lean not to our own understanding. We need to acknowledge God in all our ways and let

Him direct our paths.

SOME OF US NEED POWER BRAKES

Some of us need power brakes to help us stop doing certain things. Some of us need power brakes to help us to stop holding grudges. Some of us need power brakes to help us to stop being so critical. Some of us need power brakes to help us to stop gossiping. Some of us need power brakes to help us to stop procrastinating. Some of us need power brakes to help us to stop making excuses or blaming others for our own mistakes. Some of us need power brakes to help us to stop continuing "bad habits." Some of us need power brakes to help us to stop robbing God of His tithes and our offerings.

SOME OF US NEED TO TAKE DOWN OUR REAR-VIEW MIRROR

Some of us spend too much time looking back. Some of us spend too much time looking back on our past mistakes. Some of us spend too much time looking back at our past faults and failures. Some of us need to take down our rear-view mirror so we won't continue to look back and, because we can and should learn from our past, we can instead spend time looking to the future.

Instead of looking back, we need to look up. We need to look up and tell the Lord:

"My faith looks up to Thee. O Lamb of Calvary. Savior divine. Now hear me while I pray. Take all my sin and guilt away. And let me from this day. Be wholly Thine." [1]

One of the problems with looking back is that looking back can be the first step to going back. Jesus said: "No one who puts his hand to

---

1   The New National Baptist Hymnal (Nashville, TN: National Baptist Pub. Board, 1981).

the plow and looks back is fit for service in the kingdom of God." (Luke 9:62, NIV). That's why the Apostle Paul says that he is "Forgetting what is behind and straining toward what is ahead, I press on toward the goal to win the prize for which God has called me heavenward in Christ Jesus." (Philippians 3:13-14, NIV)

CONCLUSION

There are times when all of us need a spiritual overhaul. There are times when all of us need a new engine. There are times when all of us need new spark plugs. There are times when all of us need power steering. There are times when all of us need power brakes. There are times when all of us need to take down our rear-view mirror.

There are times when all of us need to do all of this, but we can't do this on our own. We need help. Therefore, in order to receive the spiritual overhaul that we need we need to ask the Lord for His help. When you realize that you need help, you need to:

"Ask the Savior to help you.
Comfort, strengthen and keep you.
He is willing to aid you. He will carry you through!"[2]

---

2   Ibid.

BIBLICAL PRINCIPLES FOR BETTER LIVING

QUESTIONS FOR REFLECTION & ACTION

After reading this sermon:

1. In what areas of your life do you need a spiritual overhaul?
2. What has caused you to be in this condition?
3. What will you do about this?
4. When will you start?

ADVANTAGE OF DISADVANTAGES

2 Corinthians 12:7-12 (NIV)

In 2 Corinthians 12:1-6, the Apostle Paul talks about his incredible revelations. In verses 7 through 12 Paul says:

> *To keep me from becoming conceited because of these surpassingly great revelations, there was given to me a thorn in my flesh, a messenger of Satan, to torment me. Three times I pleaded with the Lord to take it away from me. But He said to me: 'My grace is sufficient for you, for my power is made perfect in weakness.' Therefore, I will boast all the more gladly about my weaknesses, so that Christ's power may rest on me. That is why, for Christ's sake, I delight in weaknesses, in insults, in hardships, in persecution, in difficulties. For when I am weak, then I am strong. (NIV)*

In making this statement Paul is asserting that there can be advantages in disadvantages.

Advantages in disadvantages? On the surface this sounds like a contradiction. How can a disadvantage be an advantage? On the surface this really does sound like a contradiction. However, on closer examination, we can see how this is possible. On closer examination, we will see how it is possible for a disadvantage to become an advantage.

Such was the case for Paul. For Paul, his disadvantages became advantages. In these verses, Paul refers to his hardships, his difficulties, his weaknesses, his persecutions as his "thorn in the flesh." Then he makes the incredible statement: "For when I am weak, then I am strong." (v.12)

Disadvantages Can Help You Develop Patience

Disadvantages helped Job develop patience. It was because of his disadvantages and the calamities that took place in his life that Job developed patience.

BIBLICAL PRINCIPLES FOR BETTER LIVING

According to the Scriptures, Satan was convinced that Job trusted God because God had blessed him with great wealth. God had blessed Job with servants. God had blessed Job with property. God had blessed Job with seven sons and three daughters.

Satan was convinced that Job trusted God because God had "put a hedge around him and his household and everything he has" (Job 1:10 NIV). Satan was convinced that it was because of these "advantages" that Job trusted God. Therefore, Satan challenged God to remove this "hedge" because he believed that without these advantages Job would curse God to his face.

According to the Scriptures, the Lord God accepted Satan's challenge and allowed Satan to attack Job's wealth and his family. God even allowed Satan to attack Job's health.

Satan was convinced that those disadvantages would destroy Job's faith and cause him to turn away from God.

When some of Job's property was stolen and other property was destroyed, Satan was convinced that those events would cause Job to lose his faith and turn away from God. When Job's ten children were killed by a natural disaster, Satan was convinced that this could cause Job to lose his faith a and turn away from God. When the Lord God allowed Satan to attack Job's body and Job lost his health, Satan was convinced that this would cause Job to lose his faith and turn away from God. When Satan attacked Job's wife and caused her to tell Job to "curse God and die," Satan was convinced that this would cause Job to lose his faith and turn away from God.

These were physical, emotional, and spiritual "disadvantages" that Satan was convinced would cause Job to lose his faith and turn away from God.

Instead of causing Job to lose his faith and his confidence in God, Job developed great patience. In spite of his negative situation, Job was willing to wait on God. In spite of his negative situation, Job was willing to say, *"All the days of my appointed time I will wait until my change comes"* (Job 14:14 KJV). In spite of his negative situation, Job was willing to continue to trust God because he was willing to say, *"Though He slay me, yet will I trust Him"* (Job 13:15 KJV). In spite of his negative situation, Job was willing to continue to worship God because he was willing to say: *"The Lord gave and the Lord has taken away; may the name of the Lord be praised.* (Job 1:21 NIV)

Disadvantages can help you develop patience. Disadvantages can help you to develop the patience to wait on God. Disadvantages can help you develop the patience to trust God in spite of your situation and your circumstances. Disadvantages can help you develop patience and trust God when "all hell is breaking loose in your life."

Disadvantages Can Help You Rely on God's Grace

In 2 Corinthians 12, the Apostle Paul complains about his thorn in the flesh. Paul says that his thorn in the flesh was a blessing from God to keep him from becoming conceited because of the great revelations he had received from God. After pleading with the Lord three times to take away the thorn, the Lord God told him: *"My grace is sufficient for you, for my power is made perfect in weakness"* (2 Cor. 12:9 NIV). In light of that revelation from the Lord, Paul was able to say:

Therefore, I will boast all the more gladly in my weaknesses, so that Christ's Power may rest on me. That is why, for Christ's sake, I delight in weaknesses, in insults, in hardships, in persecutions, in difficulties. For when I am weak, then I am strong. (2 Corinthians 12:10 NIV)

As a result of the hardships and difficulties he faced because of his thorn in the flesh, Paul was instructed and encouraged to rely on God's grace.

As we face the ups and downs of life and the hardships and difficulties, they can help us rely on God's grace. As we face the trials and tribulations

BIBLICAL PRINCIPLES FOR BETTER LIVING

of life, they can help us rely on God's grace. As we face setbacks and disappointments, they can remind us and help us to rely on God's grace.

The Lord God told the Apostle Paul that *"My grace is sufficient for you, for my power is made perfect in weakness." (2 Corinthians 12:9, NIV)*

We need to realize and affirm that God's grace is sufficient for us. Whatever we're going through, God's grace is sufficient.

Sometimes I say to people: "I'd rather have cancer and God's grace, than not have cancer and not have God's grace."

To know that God's power is made perfect in weakness is to know that the more I am willing to admit my weakness and rely on His power, the more of God's power is given to me.

Disadvantages Can Help You Grow

Paul's disadvantages helped him to grow. Paul's disadvantages helped him to grow because he says, *"When I am weak, then I am strong." (12:10)*

In making this statement, Paul is saying that when he acknowledges his weakness, he is acknowledging his dependence on God. Paul is saying that when he acknowledges his dependence on God, God gives him the strength that he needs.

Hardships and difficulties can help you grow. Disappointments and setbacks can help you grow. Trials and tribulations can help you grow. Disadvantages can help you grow.

It is doubtful that Helen Keller would have become the person that she was if it were not for her perceived disabilities.

After becoming deaf and blind at the age of 18 months, it looked as though this would be a lasting disadvantage. However, remarkable teacher and mentor, Ann Sullivan, helped her to develop the skills and the abilities to rise above those conditions and make great contributions to our society and to the world.

Everything that looks like and is intended to have negative consequences doesn't always work out that way.

GOD FIRST

When Joseph's brother sold him into slavery, they thought that would be the end of him. They thought he would live the rest of his life as a slave and die as a slave. They had no idea that God had a purpose for Joseph's life, and that nothing could prevent it from being accomplished. They had no idea that Joseph would be imprisoned for the lie of Potiphar's wife and would be in the right place, at the right time to be brought to Pharaoh's attention so that he could interpret the dream that enabled Pharaoh and the people of Egypt to prepare for the coming famine. Joseph's brothers had no idea that they would have to come to Egypt and buy grain from the brother they had sold into slavery. When they discovered this and feared for their lives, Joseph told them that he was forgiving them because although they meant it for evil *"God meant it for good"* (Gen. 50:20 NKJV).

Although it may seem like a contradiction, there can be advantages in disadvantages. Therefore, the next time you're in a negative situation, talk to yourself. The next time you have to face some trial or tribulation, a disappointment or setback, or experience something that you perceive as a disadvantage, talk to yourself. When you talk to yourself, say to yourself—in the words of one of our African American songs of faith: Through It All.

> *I've had many tears and sorrows. I've had questions for tomorrow. There's been times I didn't know right from wrong. But in every situation. God gave me blessed consolation, that my trials come to only make me strong. Through it all. Through it all. I've learned to trust in Jesus. I've learned to trust in God. Through it all, I've learned to depend upon His Word. I've been to lots of places. I've seen lots of faces. There's been times I felt so all alone. But in my lonely hours. Yes, those precious lonely hours. Jesus let me know that I was His own. Through it all. Through it all. I've learned to trust in Jesus. I've learned to trust in God. Through it all, I've learned to depend upon His Word. I thank God for the mountains,*

BIBLICAL PRINCIPLES FOR BETTER LIVING

and I thank Him for the valleys. I thank Him for the storms He brought me through. For if I'd never had a problem. I wouldn't know that God could solve them. I'd never know what faith in God can do. Through it all, I've learned to trust in Jesus. Through it all, I've learned to trust In God. Through it all, I've learned to depend upon His Word.[3]

QUESTIONS FOR REFLECTION & ACTION
After reading this sermon:

1. What has been the unexpected benefit of some of the negative experiences in your life?
2. What have you learned from these experiences?
3. How has those lessons helped you develop your spiritual character?
4. How have you learned to view "negative experiences?"

---

3   (*Through It All.* Crouch, Andrae'. Manna Music, 1971)

ESSENTIALS FOR SPIRITUAL GROWTH
2 Peter 1:3-9 (NIV)

INTRODUCTION

Do you want to be a better person? Do you want to be more like Jesus? If so, you have to *continue* to grow spiritually. In order to continue to grow spiritually, there are some things that you have to do.

In our text, the Apostle Peter tells us some specific things that we need to do in order to continue to grow spiritually.

ADD TO YOUR FAITH GOODNESS
The Apostle Peter tells us to "add to your faith goodness."

Goodness (spiritual goodness) is *not* something that we produce on our own. Spiritual goodness is *not* something we achieve through our own efforts. Spiritual goodness is produced in us *by* the Holy Spirit.

The Scripture says: *"Not by might (human might), nor by power (human power). but by My Spirit,* says the Lord of hosts." (Zechariah 4:6, KJV)

Jesus said: *"You will receive power when the Holy Spirit comes on you; and you will be my witnesses in Jerusalem, and in all in Judea and Samaria, and to the ends of the earth." (Acts 1:8, NIV)*

Spiritual goodness is produced *by* the Holy Spirit. Spiritual goodness is produced in us *by* the Holy Spirit. The Holy Spirit *helps us* to become more like Jesus so that we can develop good character. As we develop *good character*, we develop *good thoughts* that lead to doing *good deeds*. Therefore, *spiritual goodness* is *goodness* that we develop *through* the Holy Spirit.

ADD TO GOODNESS KNOWLEDGE
The Apostle Peter tells us to add *knowledge* to our spiritual goodness.

By knowledge the Apostle Peter is *not* talking about human knowledge. He is *not* talking about physical knowledge. He is *not* talking about scientific knowledge. He is talking about is *spiritual* knowledge.

Spiritual knowledge is found in God's Word. In order to increase your spiritual knowledge, you have to increase your knowledge of God's Word. In order to increase your spiritual knowledge, you need to *read* God's Word. In order to increase your spiritual knowledge, you need to *study* God's Word. In order to increase your spiritual knowledge, you need to *meditate* on God's Word. You need to do this *every day*.

Just as you feed your body *every day*, you need to feed your soul *every day*. You need to feed you spirit *every day*. You need to feed on God's Word *every day*.

On a daily basis, how much time do you spend *reading* God's Word? How much time do you spend *studying* God's Word? How much time do you spend *meditating* on God's Word? How much time do you spend *discussing* God's Word? How much time do you spend *sharing* God's Word? The *more* you do so, the *more* you will grow spiritually!

ADD TO KNOWLEDGE SELF-CONTROL
The Apostle Peter tells us to add to spiritual knowledge *self-control.*

Self-control is *not* controlling yourself. Why? Because you *can't* control yourself. It's *humanly impossible* to control yourself. You *can't* control yourself. I *can't* control myself. *Nobody* can control himself.

The Apostle Paul understood that. He realized that he couldn't control himself. That's why he says, *"I have the desire to do what is good but cannot carry it out. For what I do is not the good I want to do; no, the evil that I do not want to do—this I keep on doing"." (Romans 7:19, NIV)*

There's *a war* going on. There's *a war* going on between the physical and the spiritual. There's *a war* going on between the godly and the ungodly. There's *a war* going on between the holy and the unholy.

GOD FIRST

Therefore, in our text, the Apostle Peter is telling us to add self-control by *putting ourselves under the control of the Holy Spirit.*

When we put ourselves under the control of the Holy Spirit, The Holy Spirit *helps us* do what we need to do. The Holy Spirit *helps us* control our *thoughts*. The Holy Spirit *helps us* control our *actions*.

ADD TO SELF CONTROL PERSEVERANCE
The Apostle Peter tells us to add perseverance to self-control

To persevere is to *continue*. To persevere is to *not give up*. To persevere is to *keep going*. To persevere is to *not quit*. To persevere is to *not stop*.

ILLUSTRATION

One of the best lessons that I learned about perseverance was in my first year of college when I decided to run track. I wasn't a good runner, but I liked to run.

The coach decided to enter our team in the San Jose Invitational, which included some of the best runners in the world.

I decided to run the 880. The pace was so fast that I sprained my ankle in the first few yards and had to drop out.

Later, my ankle was still a little sore, but I decided to run the two-mile just for the exercise. There were about fifty runners in this race. The first six runners to finish *placed*. I wasn't interested in placing, I just wanted to be able to say that I ran in the San Jose Invitational.

Well, the pace was so fast that half of the runners dropped out after the first mile. During the second mile, all of the runners dropped out except six. I was number six.

In order to place, all I had to do was finish the race.

When I started the last lap, not only were my team mates cheering—the whole crowd was cheering —although I had already been lapped twice.

When I came across the finish line, the whole crowd was cheering. They cheered for me because *I STAYED IN THE RACE!*

IF you want to *continue* your spiritual growth, you have to *stay in the race.*

THE ENEMY wants you to quit. *THE ENEMY* wants you to give up. *The Enemy* wants you to stop. *The Enemy* wants you to *stop* trusting God. *The Enemy* wants you to *stop* obeying God. *The Enemy* wants you to *stop* worshipping God. *The Enemy* wants you to *stop* praising God. *The Enemy* wants you to *stop* serving God. *The Enemy* wants you to *stop* reading God's Word. *The Enemy* wants you to *stop* studying God's Word. *The Enemy* wants you to *stop* meditating on God's Word. *The Enemy* wants you to *stop* living by God's Word.

IF you stay in the race, there will be a *"whole cloud of witnesses"* cheering you on. There will be a *"whole cloud of witnesses"* waiting for you at the finish line.

Abraham, Isaac and Jacob will be at the finish line. Ruth, Esther, and Naomi will be at the finish line. Shadrach, Meshach and Abednego will be at the finish line. Isaiah and Jeremiah will be at the finish line. Ezekiel and Daniel will be at the finish line. Mary and Joseph will be at the finish line. All of Jesus' disciples will be at the finish line. The Apostle Paul will be at the finish line.

Somebody else will be at the finish line.

The Rose of Sharon will be at the finish line. The Lily of the Valley will be at the finish line. The Wonderful Counselor will be at the finish line. The Mighty God will be at the finish line. The Everlasting Father will be at the finish line. The Prince of Peace will be at the finish line.

The One who went to the Cross will be at the finish line. The One who suffered on the Cross will be at the finish line. The One who died on the Cross will be at the finish line. The One who died for your sins will be at the finish line. The One who died for my sins will be at the finish line. The One who died for the sins of the world will be at the finish line.

The One who rose again on Resurrection morning will be at the finish line. The One who said: *"All power of heaven and earth is in My hands"* will be at the finish line. The One who ascended back to heaven will be at the finish line. The One who's coming back again will be at the finish line.

If you want to continue your spiritual growth, you have to *stay* in the race. *Don't* stop.! *Don't* quit! *Don't* give up! *Don't* drop out! *Don't* stop trusting God! *Don't* stop obeying God! *Don't* stop worshipping God! *Don't* stop praising God! *Don't* stop serving God!

WHY? Because *"The race is not to the swift or the battle to the strong."* *(Eccles. 9:11, NIV)*

IF you persevere, you will be able to say with the Apostle Paul: *"I have fought the good fight. I have finished my race. I have kept the faith. Now there is laid up for the crown of righteousness." (2 Timothy 4:7-8a, (NIV).*

Therefore, regardless of the ups and downs of life, stay in the race. Regardless of the trials and tribulations you face, stay in the race. Regardless of hardships and difficulties, stay in the race. Regardless of your weaknesses and shortcomings, stay in the race. Regardless of disappointments and setbacks, stay in the race. Don't stop! Don't quit! Don't give up!

STAY IN THE RACE!

BIBLICAL PRINCIPLES FOR BETTER LIVING

QUESTIONS FOR REFLECTION & ACTION
After reading this sermon:

1. Which of these essentials have helped you the most?
2. Which of these essentials do you need to develop?
3. Which of them will be the most difficult for you and why?
4. In light of what you have discovered, what do you plan to do?
5. When will you start?
6. What will be your first step?

GOD FIRST

GETTING RID OF EXCESS BAGGAGE
1 Peter 2:1-3 (NIV)

INTRODUCTION

Most people like to travel. Some of us like to travel light and some of us like to travel like Margaret—packing everything but the kitchen sink.

Some of us take things that we never wear. Some of us take things we never take out of our suitcase. That means: some of us over pack and carry "excess baggage."

In life, some of us are carrying "excess baggage." In life, some of us are carrying things we don't need and slow us down. Some of us carry things that weigh us down or hold us back. Some of us are carrying things that keep us for being all that God created us to be. That means, some of us are carrying some "excess baggage."

Some of us are carrying things that make us sick. Some of us are carrying things that give us high blood pressure. Some of us are carrying things that can give us a stroke. Some of us are carrying things that can give us a heart attack. Some of us are carrying things that make us sick. Some of us are carrying things that make other people sick.

If you have any *negative attitudes* toward anyone, that's *excess baggage.* If you have any *negative feelings* toward anyone, that's *excess baggage.* If there is some *unresolved conflict* you have with anyone, that's excess *baggage.* That's excess baggage that you need to get rid of.

EXPOSITION

In our text, the Apostle Peter tells us to get rid of several specific things. Let's look at *three* of the things he mentions.

The Apostle Peter tells us to:
"Get rid of all malice"

QUESTION: What is malice? MALICE is having *negative attitudes* and *negative feelings* toward someone **and** wanting to hold on to them.

52

BIBLICAL PRINCIPLES FOR BETTER LIVING

When some things happen to us, it's *natural* to get angry. It's *natural* to get upset. But it's *demonic* to hold on to those negative attitudes or feelings. It's *demonic* to hold those negative feelings.

WHY? Because WHEN you *"hold on"* to *negative attitudes* and to those *negative feelings* that means that SATAN and his demons are *controlling* you.

That's why the Apostle Paul says *"Do not let the sun go down while you are still angry."* (Eph. 4:26) That means, get rid of it as quickly as you can.

ILLUSTRATION

According to the Scriptures, King Saul had so much malice toward David that he tried to kill him. On several occasions, King Saul tried to kill David. That was demonic. Every time King Saul tried to kill David it was because SATAN was *controlling* him.

Anytime you hold malice toward another person it's because SATAN is *controlling* you. SATAN is *controlling* how you *think*. SATAN is *controlling* how you *feel*. SATAN is *controlling* how you *act*. SATAN is *controlling* how you *treat* that person. Anytime you hold malice toward another person SATAN is controlling **how** you think and feel and **what** you say and do.

IF you have any malice toward anyone, you need to get rid of it, because it's "excess baggage!"

The Apostle Peter tells us to:
"Get rid of all deceit"

QUESTION: What is deceit? DECEIT is to *deceive or mislead* someone. Some people are *"master deceivers."*

In order to get what they want, *some men* will deceive and mislead women. In order to get what they want, *some women* will deceive and mislead men.

In order to get your vote, *some politicians* will deceive you. In order to get your vote, *some politicians* will mislead you. In order to get your vote, *some politicians* will SAY almost anything. In order to get your vote, *some politicians* will DO almost anything!

We need to be honest. We need to be honest in what we say. We need to *say* what we mean and *mean* what we say.

Jesus said let your "*yes*" be "*yes*" and let your "*no*" be "no." When He said this, Jesus was telling us to *say* what we *mean* and *mean* what we *say*!

In order to live godly lives, we need to get rid of all deceit and be honest with one another. We need to *say* what we mean and *mean* what we say.

The Apostle Peter tells us to:
"Get rid of all envy"

QUESTION: What is envy? ENVY is *resenting* what someone has and *disliking* them because they have it.

Envy has a *twin brother*. Its twin brother is called *jealousy*. Envy has a *twin sister*. It's called *jealousy.*

That was the problem with Joseph and his brothers ---- Joseph's brothers *envied* him. They *envied* him because their father played favorites. They *envied* Joseph because their father dressed Joseph better than he dressed them. Their *envy* turned to *jealousy* and their *jealousy* caused them *get rid of Joseph.*

PARENTS: *Don't* play favorites with your children. *Don't* plant seeds that can cause friction among your children. *Don't* give your children a reason to *envy* each other. *Don't* give your children a reason *to be jealous* of each other. *Don't* give your children a reason *to be jealous* of each other *because* of YOUR attitude and actions.

IF you are God's child——IF you *really* trust and obey God, you will have no reason to *envy anybody*.

IF you're God's child——IF you *really* trust and obey God, you know that GOD will supply ALL of your needs and SOME of your wants.

BIBLICAL PRINCIPLES FOR BETTER LIVING

IF you *really* trust God—IF you *really* obey God. You know that GOD will *"supply all of your needs according to His riches in glory in Christ Jesus."*

WHY? Because IF you trust and obey God, you know **What God has for you is for you.** That means **nobody** can keep you from having God's blessings but you.

Deuteronomy 28:1-14 tells us that *God's blessings* are tied to *our obedience.* These verses tell us that God will bless us for obeying Him.

According to these verses, IF you trust and obey God will *send* you blessings. According to these verses, IF you trust and obey God, God will *send* you blessings you didn't even ask for. According to Malachi 3:7-10, IF you pay God HIS tithe and give God YOUR offering, GOD will open the windows of heaven and pour out blessings upon you so abundantly that you won't have room to put them.

According to Luke 6:38, *"Give, and it will be given to you. A good measure, pressed down, shaken together and running over, will be poured into your lap. For with the measure you use, give, it will be measured to you."* (NIV)

That means: IF you give the way God wants you to give, GOD will have people *giving* you blessings. GOD will have people *sending* you blessings. GOD will have people *bringing* you blessings. GOD will have people *leaving* blessings on your doorstep. GOD will have people *putting* blessing in your mailbox. GOD will have people *putting* blessings in your pocket. GOD will have people *depositing* blessings to your account.

IF you trust and obey God, GOD will bless you. GOD will bless you physically, mentally, and spiritually. GOD will bless you totally.

IF you trust and obey God, GOD will open doors for you. IF you trust and obey God, GOD will make a way for you. GOD will heal your body. GOD will save your soul. GOD will make you whole. GOD will turn negatives into positives. GOD will disrupt the Enemy's plans. GOD will enable you to tell the Enemy what Joseph said to his brothers:

"YOU intended to harm me. but God intended it for good to accomplish what is now being done, the saving of many lives." (Genesis 50:19, NIV)

CONCLUSION

IF you want to get rid of your excess baggage, you can't do it by yourself. IF you want to get rid of your excess baggage, you need help. IF you want to get rid of your excess baggage, you need to ask for help.

It's good to know where you can find help. David knew where to find help. That's why David said:

"I will lift up my eyes unto the hills—where does my help come from? My help comes from the Lord, the Maker of heaven and earth." (Psalm 121:1, NIV)

IF you want to get rid of your excess baggage you need help. IF you want to get rid of your excess baggage you need to "ASK the Savior to help you. COMFORT strengthen and keep you. HE is willing to aid you. And HE will carry you through."[4]

ON MONDAY, ask the Savior to help you. ON TUESDAY, ask the Savior to help you. ON WEDNESDAY, ask the Savior to help you. ON THURSDAY, ask the Savior to help you. ON FRIDAY, ask the Savior to help you. ON SATURDAY, ask the Savior to help you. ON SUNDAY, ask the Savior to help you. RIGHT NOW, ask the Savior to help you.

"Ask the Savior to help you. Comfort, strengthen and keep you.
He is willing to aid you. He will carry you through!"

---

4   The New National Baptist Hymnal

BIBLICAL PRINCIPLES FOR BETTER LIVING

QUESTIONS FOR REFLECTION & ACTION

After reading this sermon:

1. What excess baggage are you carrying?
2. What has kept you from getting rid of it?
3. What steps will you take to get rid of it?
4. When will you begin to take those steps?

GOOD ADVICE FROM GOD'S WORD
Proverbs 3:5-6 KJV

INTRODUCTION

There are times when all of us need advice. Sometime the advice we get is good. Sometime the advice we get is *not* so good. However, we always get good advice in God's Word.

In Proverbs 3:5-6 there is some good advice. That good advice says: *"TRUST in the Lord with all thine heart. And lean NOT unto thine own understanding. In ALL thy ways acknowledge HIM and HE shall direct thy paths." (KJV) In* these verses we have two *principles* and a *promise*.

THE FIRST PRINCIPLE
"TRUST in the Lord with ALL thine heart."

To trust God with ALL of your heart is to trust God with *every fiber* of your being. To trust God with *every fiber* of your being is to trust God COMPLETELY!!! When you trust God COMPLETELY, you are trusting God *"with all your heart."*

However, there are at least two different kinds of trust. There is *"because of* trust" and there is *"in spite of* trust."

"Because of trust" is trusting God **because** of what He has already done. *"In spite of trust"* is trusting God **in spite of** some of the things that He lets happen in your life.

BECAUSE OF TRUST

Let me illustrate this point. In my first pastorate in San Francisco, we lived in a small four-room parsonage attached to the church. There was a bathroom and kitchen downstairs and a living room and bedroom upstairs. When our son Colvin ll was about two years old, I decided to play a game with him. I took him to the top of the stairs and I walked down a few steps and told him to "jump." At first, he looked at me kind of

BIBLICAL PRINCIPLES FOR BETTER LIVING

funny. Then, he jumped. He jumped, I caught him. He enjoyed that and began to laugh. Then, I walked down several more steps and told him to jump. This time, without hesitation he jumped again and I caught him. Again, he had another big laugh.

If I had not caught him the *first* time, he would not have jumped the *second* time. He jumped the second time only *because* I caught him the *first* time. Because I caught him the first time he developed *"because of trust."* He developed *"because of trust"* because daddy caught him the first time.

When **we** trust God and He "catches" us, we begin to develop "because of trust." Every time your Spiritual Daddy catches you, you develop more "because of trust. "

IN SPITE OF TRUST

But there's also in spite of trust. We develop "in spite of trust" by trusting God **in spite of** some of the things that happen to us.

JOB developed in spite of trust.

JOB lost his family, his property, and his health. When Job's wife lost her mind and told Job to "Curse God and die" (Job 1:9, NIV) JOB demonstrated "in spite of trust." Job demonstrated "in spite of trust." Job stood on the tiptoes of faith, looked over the shoulder of hope and down the battlement of devotion and said: *"NAKED, I came from my mother's womb, and. NAKED I will depart. The LORD has given and the LORD has taken away;* ***may the name of the Lord be praised." (Job 1:21, NIV)***

JOB demonstrated "in spite of trust" when he declared: *"Though He slay me, YET will I trust in Him." (Job 13:15, KJV)*

We need to have "because of trust."
But we also need to have "in spite of trust.

WHEN you lose your job and you keep trusting God, *that's* in spite of trust. WHEN you lose your house and you keep trusting God, that's *in spite of trust.* WHEN the doctor diagnoses you with cancer and you keep trusting God, that's *in spite so trust.* WHEN the Enemy wreaks havoc in your life and "all hell" seems to be breaking loose, you need to have in spite of trust. You need to trust God in spite of the situation. You need to trust God in spite of the hardship; you need to trust God in spite of the difficulty; you need to trust god in spite of the setback. You need to have some in spite of trust.

THE SECOND PRINCIPLE
"Lean not to thine own understanding."

The second principle: "Lean not to thine own understanding." Why? Because our understanding is *limited.* Our understanding is *imperfect.* Our understanding is *incomplete.*

Because we're imperfect human beings, we can never understand anything completely. We get ourselves in trouble when we *"lean to our own understanding."*

Proverbs 14:12 tells us

"There is a way that seems right to man; but in the end
it leads to death." (NIV)

Only GOD is perfect. Only GOD *knows* everything. Only GOD *understands* anything completely.

BECAUSE God knows everything, it makes good sense to **consult** Him. BECAUSE God knows everything, it makes good sense to **ask** for His guidance. BECAUSE God knows everything, it makes good sense to **ask** for His help.

Instead of leaning to our own understanding, *"ASK the Savior to help you. Comfort, strengthen and keep you. HE is willing to aid you. And HE will carry you through!"*[5]

---

5   The New National Baptist Hymnal

THE PROMISE

*"In ALL thy ways acknowledge Him. He will DIRECT
your paths."*

Based on these two principles there is a promise. The promise is: *"In all thy ways acknowledge Him. He shall direct thy path."*

What does it mean to acknowledge God?

To acknowledge God is to acknowledge that God IS God. To acknowledge God is to acknowledge that God IS our Creator, Redeemer. Sustainer Heart-fixer. Mind-Regulator. Burden-bearer, and Way-Maker.

To acknowledge God is to acknowledge the **goodness**, **mercy**, **grace**, **holiness**, **majesty**, and **eternality** of God. To acknowledge God is to acknowledge that *"God is from everlasting to everlasting."* When you acknowledge God, you *consult* God.

According to verse six, WHEN you acknowledge God, God will "direct your path."

In other words, WHEN you acknowledge God, GOD will tell you **what** to do. WHEN you acknowledge God, GOD will tell you **when** to do it. WHEN you acknowledge God, GOD will tell you **how** to do it.

Do I have any proof of that? Is there any evidence of that?

According to the Scriptures:

WHEN Moses acknowledged God at the Red Sea, God told him **what** to do. God told **when** to do it. God told him **how** to do it. WHEN Moses acknowledged God, God told him to "stand still and see the salvation of the Lord." WHEN Moses acknowledged God at the Red Sea, God told him to stretch out his rod. WHEN Moses stretched out his rod at the Red Sea, God caused the waters to come together.

WHEN the waters came together, the children of Israel walked across on dry ground.

According to the Scriptures:

WHEN Joshua acknowledged God at Jericho, God told him **what** to do. God told him **when** to do it. God told him **how** to do it. WHEN Joshua acknowledged God, God told him to have the children of Israel to walk around wall **one time** for six days and on the seventh day to walk around **seven times and shout**. WHEN the children of Israel walked around the wall seven times and shouted, "The wall came tumbling down!"

According to the Scriptures:

WHEN Queen Esther acknowledged God in her crisis situation, God told her **what** to do. God told her **when** to do it. God told her **how** to do it. GOD told her to fast and pray and to have her maidens to do likewise. GOD told her to accentuate her beauty and go to the king's chamber unannounced—although the penalty for doing so was death—unless the king extended his scepter. When ESTHER opened the door to the king's inner chamber and stood there in all of her beauty and splendor, the king extended his scepter toward her in a gesture that said: "HONEY, WHATEVER YOU WANT, YOU'VE GOT IT!"

CONCLUSION

WHEN you **acknowledge** and **consult** God, GOD *will* **"direct your paths."** WHEN you acknowledge God, GOD *will* tell you *what* to do. WHEN you acknowledge GOD, God *will* tell you *when* to do it. WHEN you acknowledge GOD, God *will* tell you *how* to do it.

THEREFORE: *"Trust in the Lord with all thing heart. Lean not to thy own understanding. In all thy ways acknowledge HIM and HE will direct your paths." Proverbs 3:5-6 (KJV)*

BIBLICAL PRINCIPLES FOR BETTER LIVING

Who is He?

HE is the Triune God. HE is God the Father. HE is God the Son. HE is God the Holy Spirit. HE is one God expressing Himself in Three Persons. HE is the Rose of Sharon. HE is the Lily of the Valley. HE is the Bright and Morning Star. HE is the Wonderful Counselor. HE is the Mighty God. HE is the Everlasting Father. HE is the Prince of Peace.

Who is He?

HE is Ezekiel's wheel in the middle of a wheel. HE is Daniel's stone hewed out of a mountain. HE is the One born in Bethlehem. HE is the One who was baptized in the river Jordan. HE is the one who walked on the Sea of Galilee. HE is the one who stopped by a marriage feast in Cana and turned water into wine. HE is the One who took two small fish and five loaves of bread and fed 5,000 men plus women and children. HE is the one who healed the sick. HE is the One who raised the dead.

Who is He?

HE is the one who went to the Cross. HE is the one who suffered, bled and died on the Cross. HE is the one who suffered, bled, and died on the Cross for your sins. HE is the one who suffered, bled, and died on the Cross for my sins. HE is the one who suffered, bled, and died on the Cross for the sins of the world. HE is the one that the grave couldn't hold.

HE is the one who got up on resurrection morning. HE is the one who stood on resurrection ground. HE is the one who declared that "All power of heaven and earth is in my hands." HE is the one who ascended back to heaven. HE is the one who's coming back again!

Therefore, IF you want to live a better life: *"Trust in the Lord with all thine heart. Lean not to thine own understanding. In ALL thy ways acknowledge him. And he shall direct your paths."* (Proverbs 3:5-6, KJV)

QUESTIONS FOR REFLECTION & ACTION

After reading this sermon:

1. What did you learn from the advice given in this sermon?
2. Are you willing to apply this advice?
3. Are you willing to share this advice with others?
4. In what other areas of your life do you need advice and help from God's Word?

FROM HARD TIMES TO HALLELUJAH
2 Kings 7:1-20; Romans 5:1-5 (NIV)

INTRODUCTION
It has been said that
"Tough times don't last but tough people do!"

All of us have had some hard times, ups and downs, trials, tribulations, or setbacks. You may be going through some hard times right now.

If you're not experiencing some hard times right now, you probably know somebody who is. You probably know somebody who has lost his job, lost a close friend or loved one, or even who is going through or has experienced the pain of divorce.

Regardless of the cause of the situation, it's possible to go from hard times to hallelujah.

How do I know this? I know that because God's Word says so. I know that because God's Word says *"Weeping may endure for a night; but joy comes in the morning"* (Psalms 30:5) I know this because God's Word says that *"In all things God works for the good for those who love him, who have been called according to his purpose."* (Romans 8:28, NIV)

That means that it's possible to go from hard times to hallelujah. It's possible for you to go from having a "dark night" to having a joyful morning. It's possible for God to take something negative that happens in your life and turn it into a positive.

An example of being able to go from hard times to hallelujah is found in 2 Kings 7:1-20. In the previous chapter, we are told that King Ben-Hadad of Aram had besieged Samaria and that Samaria had a severe famine. In 2 Kings 7:1-20 we're told that four starving lepers decided to go to the camp of the Arameans and ask for food. They surmised that if they stayed in Samaria they would starve to death and if they went to the camp of the Arameans, they would either be given food or would be killed. They decided to take that chance and go to the camp of the

GOD FIRST

Arameans. When they got to the camp, they discovered that the Arameans had fled during the night because the Lord caused them hear chariots and believe that they were being attacked by the Hittites and the Egyptians. The lepers found the camp deserted, but with plenty of food along with much gold and silver. After they had a good meal, the lepers returned to Samaria and reported what they had found. After investigating and discovering the accuracy of the lepers' report, the people of Samaria were able to go from hard times to hallelujah because they now had plenty of food.

In order for Samaria to go from hard times to hallelujah, let's look at what the lepers did. What did the lepers do?

They Analyzed the Situation

The lepers realized that if they went into the city, they would die of starvation with the other people in the city. But if they went to the enemy's camp, they might be given food.

When you face hard times, you need to analyze your situation. You need to look at the possibilities. You need to look at the pros and the cons. You need to look at the possible alternatives and the possible consequence of each alternative.

They Made a Decision

After analyzing the situation, these lepers made a decision. They knew that if they stayed in the city, they would die of starvation. They knew that if they went to the enemy's camp and surrendered, they might be given food and they might be killed. They decided to take a chance and go to the enemy's camp.

When you face hard times, after you analyze the situation, you need to make a decision. After looking at the possibilities and weighing the pros and cons, you need to make a decision.

66

BIBLICAL PRINCIPLES FOR BETTER LIVING

They took Action

After analyzing the situation and making a decision, these four lepers took action. They went to the enemy's camp. After going to the enemy's camp, they discovered that the camp was deserted but that there was plenty of food. They discovered that there was enough food to feed them and to feed people in the city.

When you face hard times, after you analyze the situation and make a make a decision, you need to take action. After you analyze the situation and make a decision after prayerful deliberation, you need to take action. This may not be easy to do. You may still have some fears and apprehensions. But at some point, you have to take action. At some point you have to step out on faith and take action. After prayerful deliberation you need to step out on faith and trust God.

One of my favorite passages of Scripture is: *"Trust in the Lord with all thine heart. Lean not to thy own understanding. In all thy ways acknowledge Him. He will direct your path." (Prov. 3:5-6, KJV)*

That means when you consult and trust God, God will tell you **what** to do. God will tell you **when** to do it. God will tell you **how** to do it.

The children of Israel were able to go from hard times to hallelujah

The children of Israel suffered four hundred years of hard times when they were slaves in Egypt. For four hundred years, they worked in the fields. They were forced to build the pyramids and were mistreated, beaten, and even had their firstborn sons killed. After four hundred years, God sent them a deliverer. After four hundred years, God sent Moses to deliver them from their hard times. When the children of Israel were set free, they praised God. When the children of Israel were set free, they went from hard times to hallelujah.

Job was able to go from hard times to hallelujah

According to the Scriptures, Satan got God's permission to test Job. Satan got permission to test Job's faith. But Job held on to his faith. Job held on to his faith and didn't give up trusting God.

Because Job was willing to trust God in spite of all that happened to him, Job was able to go from hard times to hallelujah.

According to the Scriptures, after Job passed his tests, the Lord God gave Job TWICE as much as he had before. The Lord gave Job TWICE as much wealth. The Lord God gave Job TWICE as much property. Because of what the Lord God did for him, Job was able to go from hard times to hallelujah!

There's a lesson in there for us. There's a lesson in there for all of us. The lesson for us is:

When you pass your test, God may double your blessings! When you pass your test, YOU can expect to go from hard times to hallelujah!

In order to pass your test, you have to keep *trusting* God, *obeying* God, *worshipping* God, *praising* God, *serving* God, *glorifying* God, *edifying* God's church, *advancing* God's Kingdom.

Hard times are a part of life. At some time, all of us experience some hard times. It doesn't matter who you are. It doesn't matter whether you are a saint or a sinner, how much you pray or how much you love the Lord—you are going to have some hard times. But the good news is: IF you trust and obey God, you can go from hard times to hallelujah.

African American slaves went from hard times to hallelujah

The African slave trade lasted more than four hundred years. These were four hundred years of hard times. During these four hundred years, Black Africans were kidnapped from their homelands. Men and women were chained and shackled in close quarters during the voyage from

Africa to America. During the voyage some died of disease. Some jumped overboard.

Those who survived the journey and made it to America were sold into slavery. Families were torn apart as relatives were sold to different owners. Slaves were beaten. Some were tortured, castrated, raped, or even killed.

After the Emancipation Proclamation of 1863 that ended legal slavery in parts of certain states, some slaves were able to rejoice. For years, former slaves in some states celebrated on the 19th of June. The holiday of "Juneteenth." These former slaves were able to celebrate a "hallelujah" day each year.

You can go from hard times to hallelujah

In Romans 5:1-5, the Apostle Paul tells us how. In these verses, the Apostle Paul tells believers that because we have been justified by faith, we *"have peace with God through our Lord Jesus Christ."* And BECAUSE we have peace with God through our Lord Jesus Christ. we CAN *"rejoice in our sufferings." (NIV)*

In this statement, Paul is telling believers that in spite of sufferings, hardships, difficulties and in spite of what happens to us, we CAN go from hard times to hallelujah.

WHY? Because believers know some things.
Believers know that:
"All things work together for good for those who love the Lord,
for those who are called according to His purpose."
(Romans 8:28)

Believers know that:
"No weapon formed against us shall prosper"
(Isaiah 54:17)

GOD FIRST

Believers know that:
"Nothing can separate us from the love of God."
(Romans 8:39)

Believers know that:
"Weeping may endure for a night but joy comes in the morning."
(Psalm 30:5)

Therefore, believers can tell the enemy:
"You meant it for evil but God meant it for good!"
(Genesis 50:20)

IF you trust and obey God, YOU can go from hard times to hallelujah!
Why? Because ....
IF you're God's child, you have been *"justified by faith."*
(Rom. 5:1, KJV))

IF you're God's child, *"You have peace with God through our Lord Jesus Christ." (Rom.5:1, KJV)*

BECAUSE you've been *"justified by faith."*
BECAUSE you have *peace with God through our Lord Jesus Christ*

BECAUSE you have peace through Jesus Christ, *you can rejoice in your suffering (Rom. 5:3)*

Whatever you're going through remember that: *"Hard times don't last."* Remind yourself that: *"This too shall pass."*
Remind yourself that: *"GOD is still on the throne."*

BIBLICAL PRINCIPLES FOR BETTER LIVING

Because God is still on the throne, you know that: *"The Lord will make a way, somehow!"* Because God is still on the throne, you can tell yourself:

"Like a ship that's tossed and driven, battered by an angry sea.
When the storms of life are raging and the fury falls on me.

Sometimes I wonder what I could have done
to make this race so hard to run.
Then I say to myself don't worry take courage.
The Lord will make a way, somehow!"

"YES! the Lord will make a way somehow.
When beneath the cross I bow.
He will take away each sorrow. Let Him have your burdens now.
When the load bears down so heavy and the weight is
shown on my brow.
There's a sweet relief in knowing, the Lord will make a way,
somehow!"

QUESTIONS FOR REFLECTION & ACTION
After reading this sermon:

1. What did you learn from this sermon?
2. In what ways can and did you identify with these starving lepers?
3. How have you dealt with hard times in the past?
4. With God's help, how will you deal with hard times in the future?

GOD FIRST

CHAPTER TWO

DEALING WITH DIFFICULT THINGS

"Dealing with Doubt"
"Dealing with Disappointment"
"Dealing with Disaster"
"Dealing with Death"

DEALING WITH DOUBT

Mark 9:14-24 (NIV)

INTRODUCTION

At various times in our life, all of us have to deal with difficult things. Some of these difficult things may have been personal, physical, mental or emotional, relational, social, financial, or spiritual.

The theme for the sermons in this chapter is "Dealing with Difficult Things." The first sermon in this chapter will focus on "Dealing with Doubt."

Has your faith ever been tested? Have you ever had at least a twinge of doubt about some of God's promises? If so, you are not alone. If the truth is told, at some times in our life all of us have had some doubts. At some times in our life all of us have questioned God. Therefore, let's take a closer look at the situation in Mark 9:14-24 and see what we can learn from it.

OBSERVATION

In this passage of Scripture, a man brought his son first to the disciples of Jesus and then to Jesus Himself because his son *"had a spirit that had robbed him of his speech."* (Mk. 9:17) After chiding His disciples because they were unable to drive out this spirit, Jesus told them to *"Bring the boy to me."* (Mk. 9:19) When the boy was brought to Jesus, the spirit attacked the boy again and threw him into a convulsion. At this point, the father told Jesus that if He could do anything, *"take pity on us and help us"* (Mk. 9:22) Upon hearing this statement, Jesus told this man, *"Everything is possible to him who believes"* (Mk. 9:23) In response to this statement from Jesus, the father replied: *"I do believe; help me overcome my unbelief!"* (Mk. 9:24)

In making this statement, the man was telling Jesus that while he had faith, he also had some doubts and needed His help to overcome them.

If the truth be told, all of us are like this man. If the truth be told, those of us who have faith also have some doubts. How do we overcome this? How do we deal with our doubts that are mixed in with our faith?

Jesus gives us the clue to dealing with our doubts in verse 23. In one version of Scripture, Jesus says in this verse, *"All things are possible for him who believes."* In another version of Scripture, Jesus says in this verse, "Everything is possible for him who believes." In both of these versions of Scripture I believe that Jesus is saying to us:

If you feed your faith, your doubts will die!

The reason why doubts remain is because we continue to feed them. The reason why doubts remain is because we're not feeding our faith.

How can we feed our faith? How do we feed our faith? I believe that there are three basic ways that we can and do feed our faith.

DEALING WITH DIFFICULT THINGS

Feed Your Faith on God's Word
If you want your doubts to die, feed your faith on God's Word because it is spiritual food.

Jesus said, "Man shall not live on bread alone but on every word that comes from the mouth of God." (Matt. 4:4, NIV)

If you want your doubts to die, feed your faith on God's Word. Feed your faith by reading a good portion of God's Word every day. I encourage believers to spend at least an hour a day reading God's Word.

Feed your faith by taking advantage of as many opportunities as possible to study God's Word. After you read God's Word, spend some time meditating on what you have read.

Feed your faith by memorizing as much of God's Word as possible. Set a goal to remember a specific number of Scriptures each day. If you set a goal to memorize just one verse of Scripture a day, at the end of the year you will have memorized 365 verses of Scripture.

As you read, study, and meditate on God's Word try to focus on as many of God's promises as possible. Promises like: "I will never leave nor forsake you." (Heb. 13:5) "I will be with you always, even to the end of the age." (Matt. 28:20). "My grace is sufficient for you." (2 Cor. 12:9). "No weapon formed against you shall prosper." (Isa. 54:17, KJV). "Weeping may endure for a night, but joy comes in the morning." (Ps. 30:5, KJV) "Thou shall keep him in perfect peace who mind is stayed on thee because he trusts in Thee." (Is. 26:3, KJV). "The Lord is my light and my salvation, whom shall I fear? The Lord is the strength of my life, of whom shall I be afraid?" (Ps. 27:1) "They that wait upon the Lord shall renew their strength. They shall mount up with wings of eagles. They shall run and not be weary. They shall walk and not faint." (Is. 40:31, KJV) "What shall separate us from the love of Christ ...?" (Rom. 8:38, KJV)

Feed Your Faith on God's Record

You can feed your faith by looking at God's record. You can feed your faith by looking at what God did for others. You can feed your faith by reading what God did for Abraham, Isaac, and Jacob. You can feed your faith by reading what God did for Moses and Joshua. You can feed your faith by reading what God did for Ruth, Esther, and Naomi. You can feed your faith by reading what God did for Deborah, Sarah, and Mary.

You can feed your faith by reading what God did for the woman who was caught in adultery. You can feed your faith by looking at what God did for the woman with the issue of blood who touched the hem of His garment. You can feed your faith by reading what the Lord did for the woman of Samaria and for the people of Samaria. You can feed your faith by reading what the Lord did for Daniel and for Shadrach, Meshach, Abednego.

When you feed your faith by looking at God's record, you know that "There is *no secret what God can do. What He's done for others, He'll do for you. With arms wide open, He'll pardon you. There is no secret what God can do!*"

You can feed your faith by looking at what God has done for you by counting your blessings and by remembering how God has blessed you. Feed your faith by remembering how God has kept you, made a way for you and opened doors for you.

Feed your faith by remembering that God saved you, healed you, delivered you, and set you free. Feed your faith by remembering that God has performed signs and wonders and miracles and healings in your life.

God may have set you free from drugs, alcohol, pornography, racism, sexism, or discrimination.

Feed Your Faith on Songs that Strengthen Your Faith

Whatever your cultural or religious background, there are probably some songs that have or can strengthen your faith.

DEALING WITH DIFFICULT THINGS

For some of us there have been songs like:
- "A Charge to Keep I Have"
- "Amazing Grace"
- "There is a Balm in Gilead"
- "I Need Thee Every Hour"
- "Love Lifted Me"
- "It Pays to Serve Jesus"
- "Jesus is All the World to Me"
- "Precious Lord"
- "Something Within Me"
- "This Little Light of Mine"
- "If Jesus Goes with Me"
- "Peace, Be Still"
- "Just as I Am"
- "His Eye is On the Sparrow"
- "Beams of Heaven"
- "What a Friend We Have in Jesus"
- "The Lord Will Make a Way, Somehow"
- "Just a Little Talk with Jesus"
- "Through it All"
- "I Must Tell Jesus"
- "We've Come This Far by Faith"
- "Hold to God's Unchanging Hand"
- "Blessed Assurance"
- "Steal Away to Jesus"
- "My Hope is Built"
- "Satan, We're Gonna Tear Your Kingdom Down"
- "We've Come This Far by Faith"
- "O Happy Day"
- "Hold to God's Unchanging Hand"
- "It Pays to Serve Jesus"

CONCLUSION

If you want your doubts to die, feed your faith. The more you feed your faith, the more of your doubts will die. The more you feed your faith on God's Word, the more of your doubts will die.

Feed your faith by reading, meditating, memorizing, trusting, obeying, and living by God's Word daily. Feed your faith by listening to God's Word as often as you can. Why? Because the Apostle Paul says that "faith comes by hearing the word."

My prayer is that you will let your doubts die by feeding your faith with an abundance of God's Word!

QUESTIONS FOR REFLECTION & ACTION
After reading this sermon:

1. What did you learn from this message?
2. What are some of your doubts?
3. How are you dealing with them?
4. With God's help, how will you deal with them in the future?

DEALING WITH DISAPPOINTMENT
Luke 5:1-11 (NIV)

INTRODUCTION

In this second sermon on the theme "Dealing with Difficult Things," let's focus our attention on the matter of "Dealing with Disappointment."

Have you ever been disappointed? I'm sure you have been. I'm sure there have been times in your life when things didn't turn out the way you thought they would. I'm sure there have been times in your life when things didn't turn out the way you had planned. I'm sure there have been times in your life when things didn't turn out the way you hoped they would turn out. At those times, I'm sure you were disappointed and you had to deal with that disappointment.

Several years ago, in my pastorate in Gary, one of my members knew that I liked chocolate-covered almonds from Sees or from Fannie Mae, and she would sometime bring me a little bag or even a box of this candy. One night, I was walking through the church and she was coming toward me with a box of candy in her hand. She was smiling and I smiled back at her. As I passed her in the aisle, I snatched the box of candy out of her hand, and she laughed as I did so. When I got home, I told Margaret that I had a box of candy from Dorothy and that it was all mine. When I opened the box, I got a big surprise. Instead of a box of candy, Dorothy had given me a box of dead batteries.

Needless to say, I was greatly surprised and greatly disappointed. So, I decided to call Dorothy. When she answered the phone, I didn't say anything. I just hung up. She knew the call was from me. So she called me back and burst out laughing. For me, it was no laughing matter because I was greatly disappointed.

OBSERVATION

In the story found in Luke 5:1-11, Simon Peter and his companions had been fishing all night and had not caught anything. Because they had no doubt expected to catch at least some fish, they were obviously disappointed. However, Simon Peter and his companions learned at least two important lessons. From the two lessons that they learned, we can learn two important things about dealing with disappointment.

Hard Work Does Not Prevent Disappointment

The first lesson that Simon Peter and his companions learned from this experience is that hard work does not prevent disappointment.

These men had worked and toiled all night. These men had thrown out their nets all night. These men had been expecting to catch some fish all night. Consequently, these men learned that hard work does not prevent disappointment.

That's a lesson that each of us needs to learn. Just because you work hard, doesn't guarantee that you won't be disappointed.

It is said that Thomas Edison tried some 10,000 experiments before he came up with the right formula that produced the electric light bulb.

From my own personal experience, I know that hard work doesn't prevent disappointment.

At the age of seven I got my first job picking cotton in Kemp, Texas. I was excited about going to work every day. I was even more excited about the prospect of being paid at the end of the week. I was in the field for almost 12 hours Monday through Friday, and I looked forward to getting paid on Saturday.

When Saturday came, I stood in line with the other workers, most of them were adults. At age seven, I was probably the youngest. When I went up to get my pay for my week of hard work, I was disappointed. I was disappointed because all I was given for a whole week's work was fifty cents. I was not only greatly disappointed, but I was also angry. I was so angry that I told the foreman, "I quit!"

The foreman and the other adults encouraged me not to quit but to work another week and then make up my mind as to whether to continue to pick cotton. They explained that although I had worked all week, I hadn't picked many pounds of cotton. They encouraged me to work another week and see what would happen.

Reluctantly, I decided to work another week. I was determined to pick enough pounds of cottons to make the job worth it.

The next Saturday, I was told that I had made good improvement in the number of pounds of cotton I had picked. The foreman and the others told me that they were very proud of my improvement. This time, when the foreman gave me my pay it was $1.15.

It was a great improvement, but I was still somewhat disappointed. In two weeks, I had worked all day for ten days and had earned only $1.65. So, at the age of seven, because of my disappointment, I decided to retire from picking cotton. And, at the age of seven, I learned that hard work does not prevent disappointment.

Doing What the Lord Tells You to Do
Turns Disappointment into Astonishment

There was a second lesson that Simon Peter and his companions learned that day. The second lesson was even more important than the first one. The second lesson that they learned was: Doing what the Lord tells you to do turns disappointment into astonishment.

When the Lord appeared on the scene, Simon Peter and his companions were getting ready to quit fishing and go home. After all, they had "toiled all night and caught nothing." But Jesus said to Peter, "Put out into deep water, and let down the nets for a catch." (Lk. 5:4, NIV). In response, Simon Peter said to Jesus: "Master, we've worked hard all night and haven't caught anything. But, because you say so, I will let down the nets." (Lk. 5:5)

In the next verses, we're told what happened as a result of doing what the Lord told them to do.

GOD FIRST

*When they had done so, they caught such a large number of fish
that their nets began to break. So they signaled their partners in
the other boat to come and help them, and they came and filled
both boats so full that they began to sink When Simon Peter saw
this, he fell at Jesus' knees and said, "Go away from me, Lord, for
I am a sinful man." For he and his companions were astonished at
the catch of fish they had taken. (verses 6–9)*

When you do what the Lord tells you to do, your disappointment
will turn to astonishment.

You need to be reasonably sure that it is the Lord who is speaking to
you and you need to be able to discern what the Lord is saying. That's why
when you believe that the Lord is telling you to do something you need as
much confirmation as possible. You need to be as sure as possible that the
Lord is telling you this.

When it comes to things of this nature, I ask the Lord for confirmation.
I ask the Lord to confirm through a Scripture or through a person or
through a "fleece."

To get an understanding of the concept of the "fleece," I encourage
you to read what Gideon did in Judges 6:36-40.

Every day, people ask the Lord to bless them. Every day, someone asks
the Lord to bless them with a job, a home, a promotion, or an increase in
their finances. Instead of asking the Lord to bless peoples' finances, I tell
them to do what the Lord has already told them to do in Deuteronomy
28:1-14, in Malachi 3:7-10, in Matthew 6:25-34, in Luke 6:38, and in 2
Corinthians 8 and 9.

In Deuteronomy 28:1-14, the Lord promises that when you "obey
Him" He will "send his blessings" on you without you asking.

In Malachi 3:7-10, the Lord promises that if you trust and obey Him
by returning to Him "His tithe" (ten percent of your income) plus "your
offering" (your freewill gift of gratitude to God above His tithe) He will

"open the windows of heaven and pour out blessings so abundantly that you will not have room enough to receive them."

In Matthew 6:25-33, the Lord tells us to not worry about the necessities of life——what we will eat, drink and wear—but to *"Seek first the kingdom of God and His righteousness and all these things will be given to you as well." (v. 33, NIV)*

In Luke 6:38, the Lord says: *"Give, and it will be given to you. A good measure, pressed down, shaken together and running over, will be poured into your lap. For with the same measure you use, it will be measured to you." (NIV)*

The entire chapters of 2 Corinthians 8 and 9 deal with the relationship between giving and receiving blessings. In 2 Corinthians 8, generosity is encouraged. In 2 Corinthians, we are encouraged to sow generously. 2 Corinthians 9:10-11 says:

"Now he who supplies seed to the sower and bread for food will also enlarge the harvest of your righteousness. You will be made rich in every way so that you can be generous on every occasion, and through us your generosity will result in thanksgiving to God." (NIV)

When you do these and other things that the Lord tells you to do, you won't have to ask the Lord for a financial blessing. The Lord promises that they will come to you automatically because of your faith and trust based upon your correct priorities.

CONCLUSION

Simon Peter and his companions had to deal with the disappointment of toiling all night and catching no fish. From their experience that night, they learned two very important lessons. They learned that hard work doesn't prevent disappointment. They also learned that when you do what the Lord tells you to do, your disappointment will turn to astonishment. Hopefully, each of us will learn these same lessons.

QUESTIONS FOR REFLECTION & ACTION

After reading this sermon:

1. What did you learn from this sermon?
2. What have been some of your greatest disappointments?
3. How have you dealt with them?
4. With God's help, how will you deal with them in the future?

DEALING WITH DISASTER
Job 1:13-21 (NIV)

INTRODUCTION

In this third sermon in the series on the theme "Dealing with Difficult Things," let's focus our attention on the matter of "Dealing with Disaster."

On Friday, November 22, 1963, disaster struck our nation when President John Fitzgerald Kennedy was assassinated in Dallas, Texas. And as a result, the nation and the world had to deal with this terrible disaster.

On Tuesday, September 11, 2001, disaster struck our nation again when terrorists took over airplanes and ran into the Empire State Building and the Pentagon. That created a disaster that still affects our nation and the world.

OBSERVATION

Disasters are a part of life. Every day a disaster of some kind takes place somewhere in the world. When disasters strike, we cannot always run and hide. Even if and when we are able to run and hide, we still have to deal with the aftermath of these disasters.

How do you handle or deal with disasters? What do you do when disasters strike in your life? What do you do when a disaster strikes your family or the city in which you live?

The story of Job is about a man who had to deal with several disasters. Therefore, let's turn our attention to the story of Job and see what we can learn from him that can help us to deal with the disaster we have to face.

OBSERVATION

According to the Scriptures, Job was a man of sorrow and was well-acquainted with grief. Job attended and graduated from the school of hard knocks. Job graduated from the University of Disaster and received a Ph.D. in patience.

According to the Scriptures, Job lost his health, his wealth, his children, his servants, his property, and livestock. Job's wife showed that she has lost her mind when she told him to "curse God and die."

OBSERVATION

According to the Scriptures, all of this happened to Job because he was being attacked by Satan. Satan had gotten permission from the Lord to test Job. Satan had gotten permission from the Lord to test Job's faith. Satan had gotten permission from the Lord to test Job's patience along with his spiritual and moral integrity.

People today are being attacked by Satan physically, mentally, financially, and spiritually.

Right now, you may be facing some disastrous situation because you're being attacked by Satan. Satan may have gotten permission from the Lord to test your faith and your spiritual and moral integrity.

Satan may have gotten permission from God to attack your health or your marriage. Satan may have even gotten permission from God to attack your children.

If you've been born into the family of God by accepting Jesus Christ as the Lord of your life and as the Savior of your soul, you're God's child. If you're God's child, Satan has to get God's permission to attack you.

When God gives Satan permission to attack one of His children, it's because God believes that they can and will bring Him glory not only by surviving the attack but also by becoming stronger as a result of the attack.

In one of the Rocky movies, Apollo Creed described Rocky as "The King of Sting" and as "The Master of Disaster."

I submit to you that because of the "sting" of sin, Satan is the real "King of Sting" and the real "Master of Disaster."

Therefore, let's take a closer look at the story of Job and see what we can learn that can help us deal with disaster. In order to deal with his disaster, Job did three basic things. Let's look at those three basic things

Job Got Up

According to this passage of Scripture, in light of his disastrous situation, the first thing that Job did is that he "got up."

Job had literally been knocked down. Job had been knocked down by the death of his children and servants, his health crisis, and the destruction of his property. On top of that, Job's wife had told him to "curse God and die." Job had been knocked down but he didn't stay down. Instead of staying down, Job got up.

The lesson from Job for all of us is:
When you get knocked down, don't stay down—GET UP!

When you get knocked down, don't throw a pity party. When you get knocked down, don't give up. When you get knocked down, don't accept being down as the new norm for you. Whatever knocks you down, don't let it keep you down.

When you get knocked down, turn to the Lord and say, in the words of one of the great songs in the African American church. "Father, I stretch my hand to Thee. No other help I know. If Thy withdraw Thy self from me. Whither shall I go?"

When you turn to the Lord in faith, the Lord will help you get up. When you turn to the Lord in faith, the Lord will pick you up. When you turn to the Lord in faith, the Lord will give you the strength to get up and keep going!

Job Worshiped God

In the midst of his trials and tribulations, Job worshiped God. In the midst of his disasters, Job worshiped God. In the midst of his hardships and difficulties, Job worshipped God.

In the midst of their hardships and difficulties, in the midst of their trials and tribulations, some people do the exact opposite. Some people stop worshiping God. Some people stop praising God. Some people stop serving God. Some people stop trusting God. Some people stop obeying God. Some people stop believing God. Some people stop believing God's Word. Some people stop believing God's promises. In the midst of their hardships and difficulties, some people literally "get mad" at God and move away from Him by cutting off any relationship with Him. These people don't know that that's a BIG MISTAKE!

These people don't know that the biggest mistake they can possibly make is to move away from God. These people don't realize that the time they need God the most is when life has knocked them down and they are at the lowest point in their life.

As difficult as it may be to do so, these people need to move toward God as never before. These people need to get as CLOSE to God as possible. These people need to worship God as never before. These people need to praise God as never before. These people need to trust God as never before. These people need to obey God as never before. These people need to "cry out" to God as never before. These people need to pray to God as never before.

These people need to follow the example of Jesus and go to their Gethsemane and pray until "sweat runs down." These people need to cry out to God as a woman cries out in child birth. These people need to **P.U.S.H.** These people need to **Pray Until Something Happens**!

If you want to deal effectively with your disaster, you need to worship God. You need to get as close to God as possible. You need to strengthen your relationship with God.

Job Put His Problems in Proper Perspective

According to the Scriptures, after Job got up and worshiped God, he put his problems in proper perspective. As Job looked at his problems, he put them in proper perspective when he said:

"Naked I came from my mother's womb, and naked I will depart. The Lord gave and the Lord has taken away; may the name of the Lord be praised." (NIV)

As Job looked at his problems, he put them in proper perspective by looking backward, by looking forward, and by looking upward.

Job was looking backward when he said
"Naked I came into the world."

In order to put your problems in proper perspective, you have to look backward. In order to put your problems in proper perspective, you have to look back at what the Lord has done from you. You need to look back and count your blessings. You need to look back and count your physical blessings. You need to look back and count your material blessings. You need to look back and count your relationship blessings. You need to look back and count your physical blessings, material blessings, relational blessings, and spiritual blessings.

Job was looking forward when he said:
"Naked I will go out."

If you want to deal effectively with your problems, you need to look forward. If you want to deal effectively with your problems, you need to have the faith to believe that the Lord is going to continue to bless you. If you want to deal effectively with your problems, you need to believe that "The Lord **will** make a way, somehow!"

Job was looking upward when he said:
"The Lord gave and the Lord has taken away;
may the name of the Lord be praised"

If you want to deal effectively with your problems, you need to look upward. If you want to deal effectively with your problems, you need to

GOD FIRST

rely on the Lord. If you want to deal effectively with your problems, you need to be willing to say:

"My faith looks up to Thee, O Lamb of Calvary. Savior Divine. Now hear me while I pray. Take all my sins away. And let me from this day. Be holy Thine."[6]

QUESTIONS FOR REFLECTION & ACTION
After reading this sermon:
1. What is the most devastating thing that has happened to you?
2. How have you been dealing with it?
3. How would you like to deal with it?
4. Where will you get the help and when will you start?

---

6   The New National Baptist Hymnal

DEALING WITH DEATH

John 11:1-6 & 17-21 (NIV)

INTRODUCTION

As we come to the final sermon on the theme "Dealing with Difficult Things," let's focus our attention on the topic "Dealing with Death."

Death is real. Sooner or later all of us will have to deal with death. It may be the death of a parent, spouse, child, sibling, relative, or friend.

Because death is real, sooner or later, all of us are going to die. When we die, those we leave behind are going to have to deal with our death. Before any of us can prepare to deal with death, we need to understand what death is.

OBSERVATION

According to the Scriptures, there are three kinds of death. There is physical death, a spiritual death, and an eternal death. According to the Scriptures, each kind of death involves some kind of **separation**.

PHYSICAL DEATH

In physical death, the spirit separates from the body. According to Genesis 2:7, when the Lord God formed man out of the dust He breathed into man "the breath of life" and "man became a living soul." That breath ("*ruah*") was God's spirit. God's spirit gave us life. At physical death, the spirit separates from the body. According to Ecclesiastes 12:7, at physical death "the body returns to the dust and the spirit returns to God, who gave it."

Several years ago, there was a televised report about an experiment that was performed to see what happened to the body at the moment of death. In this report, a dying person was monitored by cameras, scales, and other apparatus to "record" what happened at the moment of death. According to this report, at the moment of death this person's body dropped four ounces in weight and "something" was caught on camera "leaving" the body.

Some have speculated that the "something" leaving this person's body was the person's spirit and, that the "recorded" four ounces of body weight lost suggested that the person's "spirit" weighed four ounces.

Whatever one may believe about this experiment, Genesis 2:7 says that God "breathed into man the breath of life and man became a living soul" and Ecclesiastes 12:7 states that at death "the body returns to the dust as it was and the spirit returns to God who gave it."

According to the Bible, physical death involves **separation**. Physical death involves a **separation** of the spirit from the body.

John 11:1-7 and 17-27 tells us two very important things to help us prepare to deal with physical death.

PHYSICAL DEATH IS REAL

According to these and other Scriptures, physical death is real. Lazarus was dead physically. After he died, Lazarus was buried in a tomb. When Jesus arrived at Bethany, Lazarus had been in the tomb dead for four days. These verses make it clear that physical death is real.

PHYSICAL DEATH IS TEMPORARY

The second thing that these verses tell us about physical death is that physical death is temporary.

When Jesus arrived at Bethany, He had a conversation with Martha. In this conversation, Jesus tells Martha that her brother will live again. Jesus then told Martha that He is "the resurrection and the life" and whoever believes in Him will live, even though he dies and that whoever lives and believes in Him will "never die." (v. 25-26)

After telling this to Martha, Jesus went to the tomb and called Lazarus back from the dead.

I believe that Jesus was telling Martha (and is telling us) that whoever believes in him will die physically and will live again because He is "the Resurrection and the Life.

I believe that when Jesus tells Martha "whoever lives and believes in me will never die" He was telling her (and telling us) that those of us who believe in Him will die physically because our bodies will die, but we will never die spiritually because our spirits are eternal. Our bodies can die, but our spirits can "never die."

SPIRITUAL DEATH

In spiritual death, a person is separated from God. A person who refuses to have a personal relationship with God is "spiritually dead." A person chooses to not trust and obey God is "spiritually dead."

That's what happened to the Prodigal Son. In the parable of the Prodigal Son, the father represents God. The Prodigal Son did not want to continue to have a relationship with his father because he wanted to be on his own and do his own thing. This son didn't want to be under the authority of his father. This son did not want to be under the influence of his father. This son didn't want to be under the protection of his father. This son did not want to be accountable to his father. This son wanted to get far away from his father. That's why he "went to a far country."

By separating himself from his father, this son died spiritually. By not having a personal relationship with his father, this son died spiritually. This becomes clear when this son repented and returned home.

When the Prodigal Son returned home, his father welcomed him and threw a party to celebrate his return. The father said to his servants,

*"Bring the fatted calf and kill it. Let's have a feast and celebrate. For this son of mine **was dead** and **is alive again**; he was lost and is found." So they began to celebrate." (v. 23-24)*

But the older son resented this. The older son resented this so much that he refused to go in and join the party. He complained to his father that although he had served him faithfully all this time, he had never thrown a party for him.

This older son went on to say, *"But when **this son of yours** who has squandered your property with prostitutes comes home, you kill the fatted calf for him!"* (v.30)

But the father told the older son, "we have to celebrate and be glad, because **this brother of yours was dead** and is **now alive**." (v 32.)

The Prodigal Son was **alive physically**, but he was **dead spiritually** until he repented and returned to his father.

This is what happens when anyone repents and returns to the Father. He goes from being **spiritually dead** to being spiritually alive.

ETERNAL DEATH

According to the Scriptures, there is also an eternal death. The eternal death is referred to in the book of Revelation as "the second death" (20:6 and 20:14). A reading of this entire chapter will help to put this in proper perspective.

It is evident from verse ten that the second death is eternal for Satan and for all who rebel against God and refuse to receive God's salvation. This verse says:

And the devil, who deceived them, was thrown into the lake of burning sulfur, where the beast and the false prophets had been thrown. They will be tormented day and night for ever and ever. (v. 10, NIV)

CONCLUSION

According to the Scriptures, there are three kinds of death and each kind involves separation. Physical deal involves a separation of the spirit from the body. Spiritual death involves being separated from God by not

DEALING WITH DIFFICULT THINGS

having a personal relationship with God through Jesus Christ. Eternal death is the death that separates one from God for all eternity.

There is much that we don't understands about either of these deaths. Yet, there is something that most people can understand and should appreciate.

Most people understand that physical death is real because they see evidence of this almost every day. Most people understand that one day they are going to die. People who understand this should appreciate the fact that God sent His Son to die for the sins of the world so that they could have eternal life.

My prayer is that every man and woman and every boy and girl will open their heart and mind and allow the Holy Spirit to lead them to a saving knowledge of God through Jesus Christ. My prayer is that every man and woman and every boy and girl will allow the Holy Spirit to convince them that *"God so loved the world that He gave His only begotten Son. That whoever believes in Him shall not perish, but have everlasting life."*

Those who allow the Holy Spirit to do this will become disciples (students, learners, followers) of Jesus Christ and disciple makers for Jesus Christ by encouraging and helping others to accept Jesus Christ as their Lord and Savior.

When this happens, they will let the Holy Spirit help them to spend the rest of their life doing things to glorify God, to edify His church, and to advance His kingdom. Then, when death knocks on their door, they will be able to say as did the Apostle Paul:

> *"The time has come for my departure. I have fought the good fight, I have finished my race, I have kept the faith. Now there is in store for me a crown of righteousness, which the Lord, the righteous judge, will award me on that day—and not only*

*to me, but also to all who have longed for His appearing."
(2 Timothy 4:6–8, NIV)*

QUESTIONS FOR REFLECTION & ACTION
After reading this sermon:

1. Whose death have you had difficulty dealing with?
2. Why has this been so difficult?
3. What do you plan to do about it?
4. What are you doing (or what are you going to do) to prepare for your own death?

CHAPTER THREE

HELP FOR THE CHRISTIAN HOME

"Help for Christian Couples"
"Help for Christian Parents"
"Help for Christian Children"
"Help for Christian Mothers"
"Help for Christian Fathers"
"Building Your Home on a Strong Foundation"
"From the Pig Pen to the Father's House"

HELP FOR CHRISTIAN COUPLES
Ephesians 5:21-33

INTRODUCTION

The first message on "Help for the Christian Home" is on "Help for Christian Couples."

Every day, couples stand before an official and promise to remain together, *"For better, for worse, for richer, for poorer. In sickness and in heath, as long as we both shall live."* However, in a few years half of these couples get a divorce. It is reported that among couples that profess to be Christians, the number is more than 50%. Furthermore, it is estimated that half of the couples who don't get a divorce have considered doing so.

From these and other statistics it is obvious that there is a problem. From these and other statistics it is obvious that all couples need help and that Christian couples need help even more.

OBSERVATION

Why do so many couples get divorced? Why do so many couples who profess to be Christians get a divorce?

Obviously, there are many reasons. Some of the main reasons why couples get divorced are: infidelity, unrealistic expectations, and marrying the wrong person.

When one partner has an affair, many marriages are destroyed. The injured party is always disappointed and often devastated. Some marriages are able to survive this, but many marriages don't survive it.

A more prevalent reason why some couples get divorced is that they enter marriage with unrealistic expectations.

People who plan to marry need to be honest with themselves and with the person they plan to marry about what they expect in and from the marriage. They need to discuss openly and honestly what they expect of themselves and what they expect of the other person. Because may couples don't do this they enter marriage with unrealistic expectations. And, when those expectations are not met, the relationship begins to crumble.

It is interesting that the divorce rate among couples who have what some people see and call "disabilities" is far less than among other couples. A main reason for this is because these people don't tend to have unrealistic expectations. They are aware of their limitations and those of their spouse and are willing to accept them as they are.

Another reason why some couples get divorced is that they marry the wrong person.

Some people marry the wrong person because they put too much importance on marrying a person who **"looks"** a certain way. They tend

HELP FOR THE CHRISTIAN HOME

to marry a person primarily because of his or her looks. When the person they marry stops "looking" a certain way, they began to lose interest. When that person gains too many pounds, goes bald, or no longer looks the way they want their spouse to look, they tend to lose interest.

Some people marry the wrong person because they marry for the wrong reason. Some people for **security**. Some men and women put too much importance on the social and economic status of the person they marry. Some of these people marry because they want to marry someone who can "take care of" them. These people want "a meal ticket."

Some people marry the wrong person because they are lonely and marry someone primarily for **companionship**. If a person is interested primarily in companionship, they would do better to get a pet—or several pets.

Some people marry the wrong person because the two of them don't have the same or compatible **values**. This can be a major problem in setting and pursuing their goals and objectives as well in their personal relationship and in rearing their children.

The problem can be even worse if a couple does not share the same **spiritual beliefs**. In 2 Corinthians 6:14-18, the Apostle Paul warns us to "not be unequally yoked with unbelievers." As a pastor, I have no problem marrying people of different racial and ethnic backgrounds who have basic values in common, but I refuse to marry people with different religious beliefs.

Margaret and I have been married for more than fifty years. People often ask me what is the secret to having a long and happy marriage. My response is usually this: "**It helps to marry the right person!**"

If you marry the right person, you will want to work through the challenges of marriage. If you marry the wrong person, you will probably not be interested in doing so.

You maximize your ability to marry the right person when you seek divine guidance and wait for His answer. Some people seek divine

99

guidance but often they are not willing to wait for His answer. They would do well to follow the advice of Proverbs 3:5-6:

Trust in the Lord with all thine heart. and lean not to thy own understanding. In all thy acknowledge Him. He shall direct thy paths. (KJV)

OBSERVATION

Research shows that the two main reasons that couples give for getting a divorce is in the area of money and sex.

These may not be the most important things in a marriage, but they sure do exert a lot of influence over whether a marriage is healthy and whether a couple is happy.

Divorced couples of all ages say that financial problems were a major factor. Eighty percent of divorced couples under age 30 say that money or financial problems was the primary problem in their marriage.

If a couple is having money problems **and** sex problems their marriage probably is or soon will be in serious trouble. When a couple has problems in these two areas, problems in other areas tend to become even more serious.

The converse also tends to be true. When a couple has a good sexual relationship and is able to handle their finances well, problems in other areas of their marriage are much easier to deal with.

OBSERVATION

Married couples need help. Married couples who profess to be Christians need even more help. Why? Because of their commitment to Christ the Enemy (Satan) wants to destroy their marriage in order to destroy them and tempt them to renounce their allegiance to God and to renew their allegiance to him.

HELP FOR THE CHRISTIAN HOME

The Enemy doesn't attack people who have **not** committed their lives to Christ because he already **has** them. They are already **in** his kingdom.

The Enemy attacks people who have committed their lives to Christ because they are now a part of THE KINGDOM OF GOD and Satan wants to wreak havoc in their lives in order to get them back **into his kingdom**.

In Ephesians 5:21-33, the Apostle Paul is addressing Christian couples. What does Paul have to say to these Christian couples? Let's take a closer look at these verses to see what the Apostle Paul has to say to Christian wives and to Christian husbands.

CHRISTIAN WIVES

In verses 22 through 24, Paul addresses Christian wives. He says to them:

Wives, submit yourselves to your husbands as to the Lord. For the husband is the head of the wife as Christ is the head of the church, His body, of which He is the Savior. Now as the church submits to Christ, so also wives should submit to their husbands in everything. (NIV)

This is very controversial statement. This statement is so controversial because many readers don't realize verse 22 is based upon and is a continuation of verse 21 that speaks of mutual submission. Verse 21 says:

"Submit to one another out of reverence for Christ."

In Ephesians 5:1-21, Paul is addressing believers in general. Therefore, Paul is saying to ALL believers that we are to submit to one another by being accountable to one another. In verses 22 to 24, he addresses wives specifically. In verses 25-32, Paul addresses husbands specifically. In verse 34, Paul addresses both Christian husbands and Christian wives. *The Full Life Study Bible* explains it this way:

101

GOD FIRST

Mutual submission in Christ is a general spiritual principle. This principle is to be applied first of all to the Christian family. Submission, humility, gentleness, patience and tolerance must be characteristic of each member. The wife must submit (i.e., yield in love) to the husband's responsibility of leadership in the family.... The husband must submit to the needs of the wife in an attitude of love and self-giving. Children must submit to the authority of the parents. And parents must submit to the needs of their children and bring them up in the instruction of the Lord [7]

The wife is given the God-appointed task of helping and submitting to her husband (v. 22-24). Her duty to her husband includes love (Tit. 2:4), respect (v.33, 1 Pe. 3:1-2), assistance (Ge. 2:18), purity (Tit. 2:5); 1 Pe. 3:2); development of a gentle and quiet spirit (1 Pe. 3:4), and of being a good mother (Tit. 2:4) and homemaker (1 Tim. 2:15; 5:14; Tit. 2:

A wife's submissiveness to her husband is seen by God as an actual part of her obedience to Jesus, 'as to the Lord.'[8]

CHRISTIAN HUSBANDS

Verses 25-33 is addressed primarily to Christian husbands. This passage begins by telling husbands to "love their wives as their own bodies" (v. 28).

Many people don't know what real love is. Real love ("agape love") is self-giving and unconditional. Real love is more than a feeling. Real love is

---

7   Donald C. Stamps and J. Wesley Adams, The Full Life Study Bible: New International Version (Grand Rapids, MI: Zondervan Pub. House, 1992).

8   Ibid.

102

HELP FOR THE CHRISTIAN HOME

expressed by what one does. God is our perfect example, because He loved the world so much that He gave His Son to die for the sins of the world.

In my pre-marital counseling sessions, I always ask a couple why they want to get married. Usually, one or both of them get around to saying they want to get married because they love one another.

At that point, I write down two statements: "*I love you because I need you*" and "*I need you because I love you.*" Then I tell the couple that only one of these statements is really saying "I love you." I ask them to tell me which statement really says, "I love you" and why does it say this.

Over the years, I've gotten some very interesting answers. The answer really gets interesting when one person picks one statement and the other person picks the other statement as being the one that really says "I love you."

Some couples feel that they love each other but don't know how to express it effectively. In these pre-marital counseling sessions, couples are reminded that all of us are different and that we feel truly loved when love is expressed in a certain way. I explain to them that all of us are VISUAL, AUDITORY, and KINESTHETIC. But that we really feel loved when love is expresses in one of these ways.

People who are primarily VISUAL feel loved when they **see** it expressed by what you do. People who are primarily AUDITORY feel loved when they **hear** you **say** in a certain way that you love them. Other people are primarily KINESTHETIC and they really feel loved by the way you **touch** them in a certain way.

You can usually tell if a person is primarily VISUAL, AUDITORY, or KINESTHETIC by the words they use. People who are primarily visual will use words like "see" very often. People who are primarily auditory will use words like "hear" very often. People who are primarily kinesthetic will often use the word "feel" in expressing themselves.

Although each of us is a combination of visual, auditory, and kinesthetic, we really feel loved when love is expressed in one of these ways.

103

Married couples would do well to discover each other's "Love Strategy" and make it a point to express their love for each other in the way that communicates love most effectively.

CONCLUSION

Married couples need help. Christian couples need help even more because their marriage has been targeted by the Enemy for destruction. The Enemy is wise and knows how to destroy a society. He knows that the family is the foundation of every society. And he knows that the institution of marriage is the foundation of every family.

That's why Satan attacked the family by enticing Adam and Eve to disobey God.

Married couples need help. Married couples not only need the help and encouragement that comes from family and friends, they also need the divine supernatural help that comes from God Almighty. The good news is: Help is available!

Help is available in and through God's Word. Couples receive divine help when they read, study, trust, and obey God's Word.

Help is available through prayer. Couples receive divine help when they go to God in prayer and wait for His answer.

For many years now, Margaret and I had spent time reading a chapter in the Bible and praying together every day. Over the years, we have read through the New Testament several times, and occasionally, we also read the Psalms and the Proverbs.

We alternate reading God's Word and praying to God. Nothing that we have done in more than fifty years has helped to strengthen us and helped to strengthen our marriage more than listening to God through His Word and by talking and listening to God through prayer.

HELP FOR THE CHRISTIAN HOME

As you begin to work to strengthen your marriage,
You are encouraged to do likewise!

QUESTIONS FOR REFLECTION & ACTION
After reading this sermon:

1. What areas of your marriage need help?
2. Why is this a problem?
3. Does your spouse know that this is a problem?
4. What do you and your spouse need to do about this problem?
5. When will you start doing this?

GOD FIRST

HELP FOR CHRISTIAN PARENTS
Proverbs 22:6 KJV

INTRODUCTION

Our theme for this chapter is "Help for the Christian Home." In the previous message, we focused our attention on "Help for Christian Couples." Since most couples eventually become parents, in this message we will turn our attention to "Help for Christian Parents."

The emphasis is on the Christian home, Christian couples and Christian parents because people who are Christians are committed to Christ. Because they are committed to Christ, they are committed to knowing and doing God's will as found in God's Word.

OBSERVATION

The basic instructions for Christian parents in this message are found in Proverbs 22:6 that says:

"Train up a child in the way that he should go:
and when he is old, he will not depart from it." (KJV)

That's an awesome statement. That's an awesome statement, because it places an awesome responsibility on parents.

Training involves many things. Training involves nurturing. Training involves instructing. Training involves modeling. Training involves demonstrating.

Training involves more than just **telling** a child what he should do and how he or she should act but it includes **showing** a child what he or she should do and how he or she should act.

Some of the best lessons are not taught by precepts but are caught by example. Consequently, if you want your child to be honest, you need to be honest. If you want your child to be trustworthy, you need to be

HELP FOR THE CHRISTIAN HOME

trustworthy. If you want your child to tell the truth, you need to tell the truth. If you want your child to love the Lord, you need to love the Lord. If you want your child to worship, praise, and serve the Lord, your child should see you worshiping, praising and serving the Lord. If you want your child to trust and obey the Lord, your child should see you trusting and obeying the Lord—especially in difficult times and under difficult circumstances.

As parents, we need to let our children see us doing the things that we tell them to do. As parents, if we don't want our children to curse, swear, use profanity, drink, smoke, and do drugs, then we should not do these things. We need to set the example.

Mothers, you need to set an example, especially for your daughters. Fathers, you need to set an example, especially for your sons. Parents, we need to set the example for the principles and values we expect our children to live by and for the things we expect our children to do.

This modeling needs to be done not only by parents but also by godparents, grand-parents, step-parents, foster parents, and guardians. As parents, we need to do all that we can to not confuse our children by giving them mixed messages and exposing them to too many influential people who have different values and live by different principles.

Because our children are going to be exposed to many people who have different values and live by different principles that we espouse, we need to have our biblical values modeled and reinforced by as many people as possible.

As your child goes to school and to other places and encounters children and other people who live by different values, encourage your child to tell you about these encounters and discuss them with you. Each time your child does this you have the opportunity to *explain* why you have different values and to help *prepare* him or her for the next encounter.

"Train up a child"

The first phrase in this Scripture is "Train up a child." To train *up* means that you need to begin early and start while the child is young. To train *up* means that you begin this training as soon as the child is old enough to understand and begin instilling positive values and principles into your child before he or she begins to get exposed to negative values and principles.

As parents, we cannot afford to wait until our child goes to school before we start this training. As parents, we need to start early and continue the process as the child grows up.

"In the way he should go"

The second phrase in this Scripture is "In the way he should go." This sounds good, but how do you know how a child "should go?" What is the direction he or she should go in?

As parents, we should train our children according to the values and principles of God's Word. We should train our children to trust and obey God's Word and live by the principles of God's Word.

The most important things in God's Word that we need to teach our children are: The Ten Commandments and the teachings of Jesus found in what we know as "The Sermon on the Mount." In the Ten Commandments and in Matthew 5-7, we have a good blueprint for teaching our children how they "should go."

In The Ten Commandments, we have instructions for attitude and behavior toward God and toward others.

In "The Sermon on the Mount," we have "The Beatitudes" (the attitudes we need to have in order to be the kind of person that God intends for us to be).

In other parts of "The Sermon on the Mount" as taught by our Lord and Savior, Jesus Christ, we have instructions regarding Christian living: adultery, oaths, love for enemies, prayer, fasting, giving to the needy,

HELP FOR THE CHRISTIAN HOME

priorities, treasures in heaven, worry, judging others, a tree and its fruit, the narrow and wide gates, and the wise and foolish builders.

If you teach your children (by both precept and by example) to live by The Ten Commandments and by the teachings of Jesus in "The Sermon on the Mount" you will definitely be teaching them "the way they should go."

"When he is old, he will not depart from it"

The last phrase in this verse says: "When he is old, he will not depart from it." That's quite a statement. Some parents have taught their children the way that they should go according to God's Word and, somehow, they seem to have "departed" from it. So, what does this phrase mean? How should we interpret it to better understand it?

As I have struggled to understand this phrase, I have consulted many sources. One source that gives a simple explanation that may be helpful is found in *The Full Life Study Bible*. The following observation is made on this phrase of Proverbs 22:6.

> "He will not turn from it." The general principle is that a properly trained child will not turn from the godly ways taught by his or her parents. However, this is not an absolute guarantee that all children of God-fearing parents will remain true to God and his word. When living in an evil society where many of God's people are themselves unfaithful, the children of godly parents can be influenced to sin and give in to temptation (see Eze. 14:14-20), where God speaks of an apostasy so great that even righteous men like Noah, Daniel, and Job could not save their sons and daughters.[9]

---

9   Stamps, Donald C., and J. Wesley Adams. The Full Life Study Bible: New International Version.

After prayerful consideration, it is my belief that the phrase *"When they are old, they will not depart from it"* is a general principle that is not absolute—all of us have free choice and all of us receive influences from the Enemy that are intended to cause us to go against God's will and purpose for our lives.

Because of God's grace, this general principle holds true in many cases. One of the most outstanding examples is the case of young Augustine who was raised by a godly mother on godly principles but lived a very sinful life for several years. During those years, his mother, Monica, continued to pray for him and for his salvation. One day, Augustine turned from his sinful ways, accepted Jesus Christ as his Lord and Savior, and became a priest and eventually a bishop and a "father" of the early church.

ILLUSTRATION

A young boy was fascinated by seeing fire flies ("lightening bugs," as we called them) for the first time. As the story goes, this young boy asked his father, "What makes those fire flies light up?" The father told him to catch one and see. After several attempts, the boy was able to catch one. But in catching it, he crushed it. As the boy looked at the crushed bug in his hand, he said to his father: "Now, I know what made that bug light up." The surprised father asked his son, "How do you know what made it light up?" The boy pointed to the crushed bug in his hand and said: **"You see daddy, the stuff was in him."**

I believe that the last phrase in Proverbs 22:6 is telling us when parents put the "stuff" of God's Word into their children (by both precept and by example) there is a good chance that "they will not depart from it." And, if they do depart from it for a season, like young Augustine, if the stuff is in them, you can expect them to return.

HELP FOR THE CHRISTIAN HOME

QUESTIONS FOR REFLECTION & ACTION

After reading this sermon:

1. What did you learn from this sermon?
2. What help do you need as a Christian parent?
3. Where will you look for and find this help?
4. When will you do so?

GOD FIRST

HELP FOR CHRISTIAN CHILDREN
Ephesians 6:1-3 (NIV)

INTRODUCTION

As we continue our series of sermons on "Help for the Christian Home," let's turn our attention to "Help for Christian Children."

We have already established that the Christian home needs help. We have already established that Christian couples need help. We would now like to affirm and established that Christian children also need help.

Keep in mind that a Christian is one who has accepted Jesus Christ as his Lord and Savior and is committed to living according to God's Word. Therefore, being a Christian is both an honor and a privilege as well as a responsibility.

OBSERVATION

In this letter to the Ephesians, the Apostle Paul is writing to Christians. He is writing to Christians who are a part of the church at Ephesus. Paul is writing this letter to Christian couples, parents, and children.

In Ephesians 6:1-3, Paul gives some specific instructions to Christian children. In these verses, Paul tells Christian children what to do and why to do it. In these verses, Paul makes three statements. Let's take a closer look at these three statements of instruction.

THE FIRST STATEMENT
"Children, obey your parents in the Lord"

In verse one, the first statement of instruction that Paul makes to Christian children is: "Children obey your parents in the Lord."

Take a good look at that statement. This statement tells Christian children to obey their parents, but it also makes a specific stipulation that limits this obedience. That specific stipulation that limits the responsibility

HELP FOR THE CHRISTIAN HOME

of children to obey their parents is contained in the phrase "in the Lord."

"In the Lord," means in those ways that honor, please, and are right and found in His Word.

This phrase limits the extent of a child's responsibility to obey his or her parents making it clear that children are not obligated to obey their parents if their parents tells them to do something wrong. This phrase makes it clear that children are not obligated to obey their parents if their parents tell them to lie. This phrase makes it clear that children are not obligated to obey their parents if their parents tell them to lie, steal, or do anything that goes against God's will as found in God's Word.

Some parents tell their children to lie for them. When someone calls on the phone or knocks at the door and asks to talk with or see one of their parents, some parents have told their children to say that they are not home.

When the phone rang, one parent told her child to tell the caller that she was not home. The child did exactly that. The child told the caller, **"Mommy says she is not home!"**

Children are to obey their parents, but they are not obligated to obey their parents when their parent tell them to say something that's not true or do something that's wrong.

THE SECOND STATEMENT
"For this is right"

The second statement tells children why they should obey their parents in the Lord. The second statement says that children are to obey their parents in the Lord because "this is right."

It's right for parents to teach their children God's Word. It's right for parents to teach their children to live according to the principles and

113

values in God's Word. It's right for parents to teach their children to trust and obey God's Word. It's right for parents to teach their children to love the Lord, to serve Him and offer praise and worship to Him. It's right for parents to teach their children to love God with all their heart, soul, mind, and strength and to love others as they love themselves.

It's right for parents to teach their children (by both precept and by example) to live by the Ten Commandments, "the Golden Rule," "the Beatitudes," and "the Great Commandment" to love others. It's right for parents to teach their children (by both precept and by example) to fulfill the Great Commission of our Lord by telling others about Him and encouraging them to accept Him as their Lord and Savior and become His disciples. It's right for children to obey their parents "in the Lord."

THE THIRD STATEMENT
"Honor your father and mother"

The third statement from the Apostle Paul to Christian children is: "Honor your father and mother."

What does this mean? What does it mean to honor your father and mother? How can and should children honor their father and mother?

To honor is to respect. To honor is to show appreciation.
To honor is to please.

Children honor their parents when they respect them, show them appreciation, and please them.

Jesus is our perfect example. Jesus is our perfect example of a child honoring his parents. The Scriptures say that, as child, Jesus honored his parents by being obedient to them. As an adult, although "his time had not come," Jesus honored his mother Mary by obeying her when she wanted him to provide wine for a marriage in Cana of Galilee.

HELP FOR THE CHRISTIAN HOME

Children honor their parents when they respect them, show them appreciation and please them—when they are growing up and after they become adults.

THE FOURTH STATEMENT

"That it may go well with you and you that you may enjoy a long life on the earth"

In the fourth and final statement in this passage of Scripture, the Apostle Paul tells us why children should honor their parents. In this final statement, the Apostle Paul tells us that two things will happen to children who honor their parents.

Things may go will with them

Now, this doesn't mean that children who honor their parents will never have any problems. This doesn't mean that children who honor their parents will not have any trials and tribulations and any ups and downs in life. What it does mean is that children who honor their parents will be blessed by the Lord.

That means children who honor their parents can expect God to supply all of their needs according to His riches in glory. Children who honor their parents can expect all things to work together for good because they are expressing their love for God and that they are called according to His purpose. Children who honor their parents can expect God to lead, guide, direct and empower them. Children who honor their parents can expect God to show His pleasure by extending His favor to them.

You may enjoy a long life

According to the Apostle Paul, the second by-product and benefit from children honoring their parents is that they may receive an extended lifespan and enjoy it. Paul actually says, "That you may enjoy long life on the earth."

The emphasis in this phrase should not be placed on long life but on enjoy.

What this verse says to me is that when children honor their parents, whatever amount of time the Lord blesses them to live, He will enable they to enjoy it.

The promise here is that children who honor their parents will **enjoy** the years God gives them to live—however long it is.

Some people live 100 years, but their lives are filled with misery and pain that prevent them from enjoying those years.

It's a blessing to live a long time. It's a double blessing to enjoy it.

CONCLUSION

Whatever number of years the Lord blesses you to live on this earth, try to enjoy them. If the Lord gives you just 25 years, enjoy them. If the Lord gives you 50 years, enjoy them. If the Lord gives you 75 years, enjoy them. If the Lord give you 100 years, enjoy them. If the Lord takes your life when you are still a child or a teenager, try to enjoy them. Try to enjoy every minute of every day and thank God for whatever time He gives you. Make the most of it and you can enjoy it.

QUESTIONS FOR REFLECTION & ACTION
After reading this sermon:

1. What did you learn from this sermon?
2. What help do your children need?
3. What are you willing to do to help them?
4. When will you begin doing so?

HELP FOR CHRISTIAN MOTHERS
Matthew 15:21-28 (NIV)

INTRODUCTION

The family is in trouble. Homes are in trouble. Marriages are in trouble. Parents are in trouble. Children are in trouble. Because they are in trouble, the need help. Therefore, let's focus our attention on the theme *"Help for the Christian Home."*

WHY? Because *Christian* homes are *committed* to God's Word. Because Christian homes are committed to God's Word, this message is addressed to ALL Christian parents. This message is addressed to *Christian* parents in general but to *Christian* mothers in particular. The topic for this message will be *"Help for Christian Mothers."*

OBSERVATION

Being a parent is not easy. Being a parent is a great responsibility. Being a mother is a great responsibility. Being a father is a great responsibility. So much so that there are times when parents get *discouraged*. There are times when parents get *frustrated*. There are times when parents get *overwhelmed*. There are times when parents *feel* like giving up. There are times when parents get *feel* like giving up on their son or daughter.

In fact, some parents *do* give up. Some parents *do* give up on their children. Some parents *do* give up on their sons. Some parents *do* give up on their daughters. Some parents *give up* on their children.

However, this was NOT the case with the mother in our text. The mother in our text *refused* to give up. The mother in our text *refused* to give up on her child. The mother in our text *refused* to give up on her daughter.

Therefore, let's turn our attention to our text and see what we can learn from this mother that can help *parents* in general and *mothers* in particular. Let's see what we can learn from this mother that can help *Christian* parents in general and *Christian* mothers in particular.

According to our text, this mother did *several* things that made a difference in her child's life.

THIS MOTHER KNEW THAT HER DAUGHTER HAD A PROBLEM

According to our text, this mother *knew* that her daughter had a problem. This mother *knew* that her daughter needed help because she came to Jesus and cried out: **"Lord, Son of David, have mercy on me! My daughter is suffering terribly from demon-possession."** (v. 22, NIV)

As parents, we should *know* when our children need help. We should *know* our children well enough to *know* when they need help. We should *know* our children well enough to *know* when they have a problem.

We should know our children well enough to know when they have a *physical, mental, spiritual, or relational* problem. The mother in our text *knew* that her daughter had a problem.

THIS MOTHER SAW HER DAUGHTER'S PROBLEM
AS HER PROBLEM

According to our text, this mother saw her daughter's problem as *her* problem. Look at what she said. This mother said to Jesus: *"Lord, help ME because my daughter is demon-possessed."*

We need to realize that when our children have a problem, *WE* have a problem. WHY? Because what affects our children affects *US*. When our children have a problem, *the whole family* has a problem.

If your child has a drug problem, YOU have a problem. YOU have a problem *relating to* that child. YOU have a problem *communicating* with that child. YOU have a problem *believing* that child. YOU have a problem *trusting* that child. Therefore, your child's problem becomes your problem, too. This mother *saw* her daughter's problem as *her* problem.

HELP FOR THE CHRISTIAN HOME

THIS MOTHER BELIEVED THAT HER DAUGHTER
COULD BE HELPED

According to our text, this mother *believed* that her child could be helped. This mother *believed* that her daughter could be helped. That's why she went to Jesus.

As parents, when our children have a problem, we need to *believe* that they can be helped. As Christian parents, we need to *have faith* that our child *can* be helped.

Whatever the problem, we have to *believe* that our child can be helped. When *our son* has a problem, we need to *believe* that he can be helped. When *our daughter* has a problem, we need to *believe* that she can be helped. Whatever the problem, as Christian parents we have to *believe* that our child can be helped. This mother *believed* that her daughter could be helped. Because she believed that her daughter could be helped:

THIS MOTHER GOT HELP FOR HER DAUGHTER

According to our text, this mother *got help* for her daughter. According to our text, this mother went to *Jesus* for help. According to our text, this mother refused *to give up* until she got *help for* her daughter.

This mother went to the right source. This mother went to the right person. This mother went to the person who was *able* to help her daughter.

According to our text, WHEN Jesus saw her *faith* and *persistence*, He knew she was not going to give up. Consequently, her daughter *was healed* that same hour.

When your child needs help, you need to get them the help that they need. When your child needs help, you need to go to the right source. WHEN your child needs help, you need to go to the right person.

SOMETIMES your *doctor* is the right person. SOMETIMES your *lawyer* is the right person. Sometimes *your child's teacher* is the right person.

JESUS is *always* the Right Person. JESUS is *always* the Right Person to go to. JESUS is *always* **the right source.**

119

ILLUSTRATION

When one of our members, Devin Bowens, was a child, he had some *major* behavioral problems. Devin had major behavioral problems at home and at school. His grandfather, Bennie, had to go to the school on many occasions because of Devin's behavior. On many occasions, Devin's family asked the church for prayer. Devin kept getting in trouble, but his family didn't give up. They didn't give up on Devin.

The church didn't give up on Devin—we continued to pray. After praying for him for several years, Devin finally began to come around. His attitude began to change and his behavior began to improve.

Today, Devin is a young college student. He's doing well in school and getting good grades. He's well-adjusted and a star athlete on his basketball team. Because of his attitude and abilities, he may one day be a candidate for the NBA.

Devin is the young man he is today because his mother didn't give up. His grandparents didn't give up. The church didn't give up. We all continued to pray.

CONCLUSION

WHEN your child has a problem, you need to take it to the Lord. WHEN son has a problem, you need to take it to the Lord. WHEN your daughter has a problem, you need to take it to the Lord. WHEN your child has a problem, you need to *"take it to the Lord in prayer.*

WHEN you take it to the Lord in prayer, you need to *be persistent.* WHEN you take it to the Lord in prayer, *don't give up.* WHEN you take it to the Lord in prayer you need to P.U.S.H!

HELP FOR THE CHRISTIAN HOME

WHEN you take it to the Lord in prayer:
"PRAY UNTIL SOMETHING HAPPENS!"

WHY? Because JESUS said, *"ASK and it shall be given."*
JESUS *said, "SEEK and you shall find."*
JESUS said, *"Knock and the door shall be opened"*

When Jesus said that He meant, *"ASK and keep on asking."*
When Jesus said this He meant, "SEEK and keep on seeking."
When Jesus said this He meant, *"KNOCK and keep on knocking."*

When Jesus said this He meant, *"DON'T GIVE UP!"*
When Jesus said this, He was telling us to P.U.S.H
When Jesus said this, He was telling us to
"PRAY UNTIL SOMETHING HAPPENS!"

Therefore, when you go to the Lord in prayer:

ASK until He gives you an answer!
SEEK until He gives you a solution!
KNOCK until He opens the door!

When you go to the Lord in prayer, P.U.S.H
When you go to the Lord in prayer:
"PRAY UNTIL SOMETHING HAPPENS!"

QUESTIONS FOR REFLECTION & ACTION

After reading this sermon:

1. What did you learn from this sermon?
2. If you are a mother, what help do you need?
3. Where will you look for and find this help?
4. When will you do so?

HELP FOR CHRISTIAN FATHERS
Ephesians 6:4 NIV

INTRODUCTION

As we continue to focus on the theme "Help for the Christian Home," let's turn our attention to the topic "Help for Christian Fathers."

By definition, a Christian father is one who has accepted Jesus Christ as the Lord of his life and as the savior of his soul. In doing this, a Christian father is one who is committed to knowing and doing God's will as found in God's Word in order to fulfill God's purpose for his life.

What are the requirements for being a Christian father? Basically, there are two. Basically, there are two requirements for being a Christian father.

Being a Christian Man

Before one can be a Christian father, he must first be a Christian man. Biologically, only a man can be a father. However, a Christian father is not just a man. A Christian father is a certain kind of man. A Christian father is a man who has been saved by God's grace through his faith. A Christian father is a man who has been born again—born spiritually into the family of God. A thoroughly Christian man is a man who has been saved, sanctified, and filled with the Holy Spirit. Consequently, a Christian man is a man who has not only been **saved** by the blood of Jesus but he is also being **sanctified**—he is in the **process** of made holy by the Holy Spirit in order for him to continue to become more and more like Jesus. And a Christian man is one who has also been **filled** with the Holy Spirit so that he will be **empowered** to be an effective witness for Jesus Christ in word and deed.

Being a Christian Husband

The second pre-requisite (pre requirement) for being a Christian father is that this man needs to be a Christian husband. That means, a

Christian father should be married. A Christian father should be married to a Christian woman.

A Christian father is not a man who is just "shacking" with some woman. The Bible is clear that one should not engage in sexual relations outside of marriage. Consequently, a man may do all of the "shacking" and "sleeping around" that he wants to do before he becomes a Christian. But when he accepts Jesus Christ as the Lord of his life and as the savior of his soul, he is committed to start living his life according to God's will as found in God's Word.

Does that mean that we should expect Christian fathers (or anyone else) to be perfect?

Certainly not! The Bible says there is "none righteous, no, not one." The Bible says, "All have sinned and come short of the glory of God." The Bible also says, "If we confess our sins, He is faithful and just to forgive us of our sins and to cleanse us of all unrighteousness." The Bible says that a truly committed Christian "does not continue" in sin.

When one accepts Christ and is born into the family of God, the blood of Jesus cleanses him of all sin and unrighteousness.

To be a Christian is not to be perfect. But to be a Christian is to be committed to knowing and doing God's perfect will.

Even committed Christians sin. But when they do, they repent and ask for God's forgiveness, and continue to let the Holy Spirit help them to become more and more like Jesus.

Even the Apostle Paul had to struggle with sin. In Romans 7:14-25, Paul admits that sometime he does not do the good that he knows that he should do, but the evil that he knows he should not do. Paul then thanks God for giving him the victory over sin through his faith in and commitment to Jesus Christ.

When anyone accepts Jesus Christ as his Lord and Savior, he or she is committed to living the rest of their life according to God's will as found in God's Word.

HELP FOR THE CHRISTIAN HOME

The only perfect person to walk this earth was Jesus Christ. He was sinless but He "became sin" in order to save us. When we confess and repent of our sins, the blood of Jesus cleanses us and God "remembers our sins no more."

In the conversation with the woman caught in adultery, Jesus forgives her and tells her to "go and sin no more." Meaning, turn from your life of sin.

God is more concerned about what we do **after** we accept Christ as our Lord and Savior than He is about what we did **before** we accepted Christ as our Lord and Savior. When we sin **after** receiving our salvation and we confess and repent, the blood of Jesus cleanses us of all sin and unrighteousness.

As a pastor, I have had the opportunity to counsel men and women who have been "living together" before they decided to get married. When they decide to get married, I commend them for making that decision. Then I let them know that if they want me to perform their marriage, they have to agree to abstain from sexual relations for a specific period of time—usually one month. Couples who are committed to living according to God's Word see the value in doing this and make a commitment to God (not just to me) to abstain from further sexual relations until the honeymoon. Among other things, this commitment gives them something to look forward to in a relatively short period of time.

Now that we see what it means to be a Christian father, let's turn our attention to Ephesians 6:4. In this one verse, the Apostle Paul gives some powerful advice to Christian fathers. Let's look at what he says to Christian fathers. In this one verse, Paul tells Christian fathers what to do and what not to do.

Don't Exasperate Your Children

Paul begins by saying to Christian fathers: "Don't exasperate your children."

GOD FIRST

Paul begins by advising Christian fathers what not to do. Paul begins by advising Christian fathers to not exasperate their children.

To exasperate is to frustrate. To exasperate is to confuse. To exasperate is to irritate. To exasperate is to provoke.

There are two main things that fathers do (and sometimes well-meaning fathers do) that exasperate or frustrate their children.

Some fathers exasperate or frustrate their children by
expecting too little of them.
Some fathers exasperate or frustrate their children by
expecting too much of them.

Fathers, we need to realize that our children are unique. Each one is unique. Each of them is different. Therefore, we should not expect all of them be interested in or to like the same things. We shouldn't expect all of them to be good at the same things. But we should realize that each of them is good at something.

Fathers, don't exasperate your sons by pressuring to be an athlete because you ran track, played football, or engaged in some other sport. Watch them and listen to them to see what they are interested in and encourage them in those areas. Encourage and help them to discover and develop their God-given gifts, talents, and abilities.

Fathers, don't exasperate and frustrate your daughters by pressuring them to pursue something in which they have little or no interest. Instead of doing that, watch them and listen to them to see what they are interested in and encourage them in those areas. Encourage and help them to discover and develop their God-given gifts, talents, and abilities.

But Bring Them Up in the Training & Instruction of the Lord

Paul then advises Christian fathers what to do. Paul tells Christian fathers that they should bring up their children in the training and instruction of the Lord.

HELP FOR THE CHRISTIAN HOME

This should be obvious. This should be obvious to Christian fathers, but it isn't. How many Christian fathers realize that it's their duty and responsibility help their children to build their lives on a strong spiritual foundation? How many Christian fathers have family devotions with their wives and children? How many Christian fathers read God's Word and pray with their wives and children on a daily basis?

According to the Bible, fathers—not mothers—have the primary responsibility for teaching and training their children to live Godly lives.

The *Shema* in Deuteronomy 6:4 is the basic Scripture in Judaism. In the *Shema*, fathers are told what to do in order to help their children build their lives on a strong spiritual foundation. The context of the *Shema* is found in Deuteronomy 6:1-9. Look at what these verses tell us.

These are the commands, decrees and laws the LORD your God directed me to teach you to observe in the land that you are crossing the Jordan to possess, 2 so that you, your children and their children after them may fear the LORD your God as long as you live by keeping all his decrees and commands that I give you, and so that you may enjoy long life. 3 Hear, Israel, and be careful to obey so that it may go well with you and that you may increase greatly in a land flowing with milk and honey, just as the LORD, the God of your ancestors, promised you.

4 Hear, O Israel: The LORD our God, the LORD is one.[a] 5 Love the LORD your God with all your heart and with all your soul and with all your strength. 6 These commandments that I give you today are to be on your hearts. 7 Impress them on your children. Talk about them when you sit at home and when you walk along the road, when you lie down and when you get up. 8 Tie them as symbols on your hands and bind them on your foreheads. 9 Write them on the doorframes of your houses and on your gates. (NIV)

CONCLUSION

Fathers, this means that we have the responsibility to teach our children God's Word. We have the responsibility to teach our children the principles of God's Word. We have the responsibility to teach our children to love the Lord. We have the responsibility to teach our children to trust and obey the Lord. We have the responsibility to teach our children to worship and praise the Lord. We have the responsibility to teach our children to glorify God. We have the responsibility to teach our children to edify God's church. We have the responsibility to teach our children to advance God's kingdom.

Fathers, we have the responsibility to teach our children to build their lives on a strong spiritual foundation by knowing and doing God's will as found in God's Word.

"Fathers, don't exasperate your children; instead, bring them up in the training and instruction of the Lord."

QUESTIONS FOR REFLECTION & ACTION
After reading this sermon:

1. What did you learn from this sermon?
2. If you are a father, what help do you need?
3. Where will you look for and find this help?
4. When will you do so?

HELP FOR THE CHRISTIAN HOME

BUILDING YOUR HOME ON A STRONG FOUNDATION
Deuteronomy 6:1-9 (NIV)

INTRODUCTION

In the gospel of Matthew, Jesus tells us the parable of the wise and foolish builders. According to the parable, the wise man built his house on a rock, but the foolish man built his house on the sand. As a result, when the storm came, the wise man's house was able to stand, but the foolish man's house collapsed. The lesson from this parable is: *Build your life on a strong foundation!*

OBSERVATION

Many *homes* are in trouble because they are not being built on a strong foundation. Many *marriages* are in trouble because they are not being built on a strong foundation. Many *relationships* are in trouble because they are not being built on a strong foundation. Many *people* are in trouble because their lives are not being built on a strong foundation.

According to our text, in order for our homes (and our lives) to be built on a strong foundation, they have to be built on God's Word.

Deuteronomy 6:4-9 is known as *"The Shema."*

The *Shema* is the most important passage in the Hebrew Bible. The *Shema* is to Jews what John 3:16 is to Christians. Deuteronomy 6:4-9 gives us several principles for building our homes on a strong foundation. Let's look at those principles.

AFFIRM THE ONENESS OF GOD

According to the *Shema*, building your home on a strong foundation begins with affirming the Oneness of God. According to the *Shema*, if you want to build your home on a strong foundation you have to begin by affirming the Oneness of God.

129

The *Shema* begins with the statement:
"Hear, O Israel. The Lord our God is One."
The *Shema* begins by affirming the *Oneness* of God.

According to the Shema, God is the only God. According to the Shema, God is the only true God. According to the Shema, God is the only true and living God. That means: God is the only Creator. God is the only Redeemer. God is the only Sustainer. God is the only Heart-fixer. God is the only Mind-Regulator. God is the only Burden-Bearer. God is the only Way-Maker. God is the only God and Father of our Lord and Savior, Jesus Christ.

Building your home on a strong foundation *begins* with affirming the *Oneness* of God.

WHEN you affirm the Oneness of God, you *worship* Him only. WHEN you affirm the Oneness of God, you *serve* Him only. WHEN the children of Israel started worshiping other gods, Joshua told them: *"Choose you this day whom you will serve. But as for me and my house, we will serve the Lord."* WHEN Satan tried to get Jesus to worship him, Jesus told Satan: *"It's written. Thou shall worship the Lord thy God and Him only shall thy serve."* Therefore, building your home on a strong foundation begins with affirming the *ONENESS* of God! WHEN you affirm the Oneness of God you worship God only.

AFFIRM THE LORDSHIP OF GOD

According to the *Shema*, IF you want to build your home on a strong foundation, you need to *affirm the LORDSHIP of God*.

According to the *Shema*, "The Lord, the Lord our God is One!"

That means: IF you want to build your home on a strong foundation, God has to be the LORD of your life. God has to be the RULER of your

130

HELP FOR THE CHRISTIAN HOME

life. God has to be the MASTER of your life. God has to be NUMBER ONE in your life. God has to be the One who *"calls the shots"* in your life. Therefore, IF you want to build your home on a strong foundation, God has to be NUMBER ONE in your family! That means: Knowing and doing God's will has to be your top priority. Pleasing God has to be your top priority. WHEN Peter and John were told to stop preaching about Jesus, they told the officials: *"We can't help but speak of the things we have seen and heard."*

LOVE GOD WITH YOUR TOTAL BEING

According to the *Shema*, IF you want to build your home on a strong foundation, you need to *love God with your total being.*

The *Shema* says that you need to *"Love the Lord your God with all of your heart. With all your mind, and with all your strength."*

That means: IF you want to build your home on a strong foundation, you need to "love God with all you've got!" That means: IF you want to build our home on a strong foundation, you need to love God with your total being. That means: IF you want to build your home on a strong foundation, you need to love God with every fiber of your being.

According to the Scriptures, to love God is to *trust* God. According to the Scriptures, to love God is to *obey* God. According to the Scriptures, to love God is to *worship* God. According to the Scriptures, to love God is to *praise* God. According to the Scriptures, to love God is to *serve* God. WHEN the three Hebrew boys were threatened to be thrown into the fiery furnace for not worshiping an idol god, they told the king: *"You may throw us into the furnace but the God whom we serve is able to deliver us. Even if He doesn't deliver us, we will not bow down to your idol god"*

TEACH YOUR CHILDREN TO DO LIKEWISE

According to the *Shema*, IF you want to build your home on a strong foundation, you need to teach your children to do likewise—by what you *say* and by what you *do*.

GOD FIRST

According to the *Shema*, IF you want to build your home on a strong foundation, you need to teach your children—by what you say and by what you do—to AFFIRM the ONENESS of God. According to the *Shema*, IF you want to build your home on a strong foundation, you need to teach your children—by what you say and by what you do—to AFFIRM the LORDSHIP of God. According to the *Shema*, IF you want to build your home on a strong foundation, you need to teach your children—by what you say and by what you do—to LOVE GOD WITH THEIR TOTAL BEING.

Verses 7 through 9 of the *Shema* tells us HOW to do this. According to these verses, IF you want to build your home on a strong foundation, you need honor God's Word. You need to read and study God's Word together. You need to discuss God's Word and emphasize its importance. According to the *Shema*, you need to display and obey God's Word. You need to "IMPRESS the principles of God's Word on your children by (1) TALKING about them as you sit at home (2) By TALKING about them as you walk on the road (3) By TALKING about them when you lie down at night (4) By TALKING about them when you get up on the morning (5) By TYING them as symbols on your hands (6) By TYING THEM on your foreheads (7) By WRITING THEM on the doorframes of your house and on your gates.

<u>In other words</u>: You need to stress the importance of God's Word by reading and discussing God's Word every day. You need to stress the importance of God's Word by having Scriptures posted in prominent places INSIDE and OUTSIDE of the house.

CONCLUSION

Can you image what IMPACT God's Word would have on your family, IF you read and discussed God's Word with them every day? Can you imagine what IMPACT God's Word would have on your children, IF you read and discussed God's Word with them every day? Can you imagine what IMPACT God's Word would have on your family, IF you

132

HELP FOR THE CHRISTIAN HOME

had Scriptures displayed in prominent places INSIDE and OUTSIDE of your house?

IF you did this, God's Word would be there to REMIND each you of God's promises. God's Word would be there to WARN each of you before making wrong choices and wrong decisions. God's Word would be there to STRENGTHEN each of you when you're tempted.

GOD'S WORD would be there to remind you that:
"All things work together for good for those who love the Lord ..."
(Rom 8:28, NIV)

GOD'S WORD would be there to remind you that:
"Thou will keep him in perfect peace, whose mind is stayed on Thee. because he trusteth in thee." (Isa., 26:2, KJV)

GOD'S WORD would be there to remind you that:
"I can do all things through him who gives me strength."
(Philippians 4:13, NIV)

GOD'S WORD would be there to remind you that:
"The Lord is my Shepherd. I shall not want."
(Psalm 23:1, KJV)

GOD'S WORD would be there to remind you that:
"The Lord is my light and my salvation."
(Psalm 27:1, KJV)

GOD'S WORD would be there to remind you that God's Word
says:
"Ask and it will be given to you.
seek and you shall find; knock and
the door will be opened to you."
(Matthew 7:7, NIV)

QUESTIONS FOR REFLECTION &ACTION

After reading this sermon:

1. What did you learn from this sermon?
2. If you are a father, what help do you need?
3. Where will you look for and find this help?
4. When will you do so?

HELP FOR THE CHRISTIAN HOME

FROM THE PIG PEN TO THE FATHER'S HOUSE
Luke 15:11-24 (NIV)

INTRODUCTION

As we come to the last message in this series of sermons on the theme "Help for the Christian Home," let's turn our attention to a very popular and interesting story that can help us to learn more about how to have a Christian home. That very popular and interesting story is the story of The Prodigal Son, found in Luke 15:11-24.

As we take a closer look at this story, let's focus our attention on the topic: "From the Pig Pen to the Father's House."

As we seek to learn some lessons from this story, there are four basic questions that need to be raised and answered. Let' look at those four questions.

The First Question
"What is the pig pen?"

The first question that needs to be raised and answered is: "What is the pig pen?" Based upon the concept of and the attitude toward pigs in Judaism, the pig pen is the worst place that you can be in.

For the Jews, pigs were the worst of animals. They were regarded as unclean and unhealthy. The pig pen, the place where the pigs were placed, was the worst conceivable place to be in. Consequently, when the Prodigal Son had to feed pigs who were in the pig pen, each time he went into the pig pen he was in the worst place that he could be in.

Consequently, the pig pen for us is the worst place, the worst situation and the worst condition that we can be in. It is equivalent to having the most negative thing that we can think of to happen to us.

People who suffer from any kind of addiction are in the pig pen. People who are addicted to drugs, alcohol, or pornography are in the pig pen. People who are addicted to and are controlled by anything that is ungodly and unwholesome are in the pig pen.

135

For some people, being on welfare, being unemployed, being underemployed, going through a divorce losing their job, or being homeless is being in the pig pen. For some people, being lost in sin without a Savior is to be in the pig pen.

People who don't have God in their life are spiritually lost are in the pig pen. People who are in sin without a Savior and instead are under Satan's control are in the pig pen.

The pig pen is the worst place, the worst situation, the worst condition that you can be in. The pig pen is a place where you don't want to be and should not be.

The Second Question
"How do people end up in the pig pen?"

The second question that needs to be raised and answered is:

"How do people end up in the pig pen?"

Excluding those unfortunate situations over which people have little or no control, most people are in the pig pen for two basic reasons: wrong attitudes and wrong choices.

Wrong Attitude

People who have the wrong attitude will probably end up in the pig pen. People who have the wrong attitude toward themselves will probably end up in the pig pen.

People who think too highly of themselves will probably end up in the pig pen. People who think they are better than others, don't have to follow the rules, and demand that people cater to their every need, will probably end up in the pig pen.

Why? Because more than anything else your attitude will determine how far you go in life. Your attitude will be a major factor in how many friends you have and whether people think they can trust you.

HELP FOR THE CHRISTIAN HOME

People who have low self-esteem and a negative attitude toward themselves are a candidate for the pig pen. People like this are a candidate for the pig pen because they may do dangerous things to impress people, to make friends, to "fit in," to be accepted.

The Prodigal Son had the wrong attitude. He didn't want to live in his father's house under his father's authority, but he wanted his father's money. He couldn't wait for his father to die so he could inherit his part of his father's estate. He wanted what his father had but he didn't want a continued relationship with his father. This young man, among other things, had an attitude problem.

Wrong Choices

People who make wrong choices are a candidate for the pig pen

People who decide to do drugs are prime candidates for the pig pen because their appetite for more drugs will increase along with their willingness to do dangerous things in order to get them.

People who decide to hang out with "the wrong crowd" are candidates for the pig pen because of the power of peer pressure.

The Prodigal Son made a wrong choice. He chose to leave home before he was ready and his thinking had matured. Because he was immature and insecure, the Prodigal Son spent his money the wrong way. He spent his money on wild parties and orgies with prostitutes. The Prodigal Son ended up in the pig pen because of his attitude that led to making wrong choices and wrong decisions.

The Third Question
"What is the Father's house?"

The third question that needs to be raised and answered is:
"What is the Father's house?"

This parable teaches us that the Father's house is the best place to be in. This parable teaches us that being under the Father's roof, being under the Father's authority, being under the Father's guidance, and being under the Father's protection is the best place to be.

> To be in the Father's house is to be safe, secure, protected,
> and under His guidance and direction.

To be in the Father's house is to be saved. To be in the Father's house is to be in the process of being sanctified—to be made holy; to become more and more like Jesus. To be in the Father's house is to be where you can cultivate your relationship with Him. To be in the Father's house is to be in the best place you can possibly be.

The Fourth Question
"How do you get from the pig pen to the Father's house?"

The fourth and final question that needs to be raised and answered is: "How do you get from the pig pen to the Father's house?"

According to this parable, in order to get from the pig pen to the Father's house, the Prodigal Son had to have a change of heart, a change of mind, and a change in attitude that enabled him to have a change in direction.

The Scripture says that this young man "came to himself." Another version of this passage says that he "came to his senses." Whichever version you use it's obvious that this young man had a change of heart, a change of mind, and a change of attitude that enabled him to have a change in direction.

Evidence of these changes is reflected in in the things he said. When he got ready to leave his father's house this man said to his father "give me." The young man said to his father give me my inheritance. When this young man came to himself and returned to his father's house he said "make me." He humbled himself and said to his father, "Make me one of your hired servants, because I'm not worthy to be your son."

HELP FOR THE CHRISTIAN HOME

According to the Scriptures, the father welcomed him back home. The father threw his arms around him and kissed him. He threw a party in his honor, but the older son resented it. The father told him:

"We had to celebrate because this brother of yours was dead and is alive again. He was lost and is found." (v. 32, NIV)

CONCLUSION

At some time in our life, all of us have been in the pig pen. At some time in our life, all of us have had the wrong attitude toward ourselves, other people, or God. Because of these wrong attitudes, at some time in our life, all of us have made wrong choices and wrong decisions.

The Scriptures says, "All have sinned and have come short of the glory of God." That means, at some time, all of us have messed up. At some time, all of us have "missed the mark." At some time, all of us have made wrong choices that caused us to go in the wrong direction.

By the grace of God, we were able to get out of the pig pen. By the grace of God, we were able to get out of the pig pen because we came to ourselves.

When we came to ourselves, we stopped wallowing in the pig pen, filled with mud. When we came to ourselves, we stopped eating at the pig trough, filled with "the slop" that the pigs were eating. When we came to ourselves, we knew we could do better and decided to do better. When we came to ourselves, we decided to repent of our sins and go back to the Father's house.

If you happen to still be in the pig pen. If you happen to still be in the pig pen of some addiction, unhealthy relationship, or under Satan's control, I have good news for you.

That good news is:

"It is no secret what God can do. What He's done for others,
He'll do for you. With arms wide open. He'll pardon you.
It is no secret what God can do."[10]

QUESTIONS FOR REFLECTION & ACTION

After reading this sermon:

1. What did you learn from this sermon?
2. What person in this parable do you identify with and why?
3. Are you presently in a "pig pen?"
4. If so, why are you in it and how do you plan to get out of it?
5. Do you know anyone who is in the pig pen?
6. Are you willing to help them get out of it?
7. What will you do and when will you do it?

---

10   The New National Baptist Hymnal.

CHAPTER FOUR

DON'T GIVE UP

"Don't Give Up on God"
"Don't Give Up on Your Children"
"Don't Give Up on Your Marriage"
"Don't Give Up on Yourself"

DON'T GIVE UP ON GOD

Genesis 32:22-28 (NIV)

INTRODUCTION

As we continue to look at God's Word for guidance as we face and deal with personal and spiritual issues, the theme for this chapter is **"Don't Give Up!"**

If we're honest, there have been times in our lives when we felt like giving up. There are times when some of us felt like giving up on God. There are times when some of us felt like giving up on our marriage. There are times when some of us felt like giving up on our children. There are times when some of us felt like giving up on ourselves.

In this chapter, we have a message for each of these situations. We begin this chapter by encouraging you to **"Don't Give Up on God."**

OBSERVATION

Do you know anyone who has given up on God? Do you know anyone who has given up on trusting God? Do you know anyone who has given up on obeying God? Do you know anyone who has given up on worshiping God? Do you know anyone who has given up on praising God? Do you know anyone who has given up on praying to God? Do you know anyone who has given up on serving God?

If you do, you need to read this message carefully so that you can share it with them and encourage them.

If you are at the point where you have decided or almost decided to give up on God, you need to read this message carefully so that you can be encouraged to not give up on God.

The Scripture for this message is found in Genesis 32:22-28 and it says:

That night Jacob got up and took his two wives, his two maidservants and his seven sons and crossed the ford of the Jabbok. After he had sent them across the stream, he sent over all his possessions. So Jacob was left alone, and a man wrestled with him till daybreak. When the man saw that he could not overpower him, he touched the socket of Jacob's hip so that his hip was wrenched as he wrestled with the man.

Then the man said, "Let me go, for it is daybreak." But Jacob replied, "I will not let you go until you bless me.' The man asked, "What is your name?" "Jacob," he answered. Then the man said, "Your name will no longer be Jacob, but Israel, because you have struggled with God and with men and have overcome. (NIV)

Let's see what we can learn from a man who had some serious problems to face. Let's see what we can learn from a man who had some

DON'T GIVE UP

serious questions about whether God was going to help him, but, in the end, refused to give up on God.

Let's look at the context of his situation.

The man is Jacob. Because (with his mother's help) he had tricked his brother, Esau, out of his birthright, his brother wanted to kill him. Therefore, he had to flee for his life.

Years later, he became prosperous, had a large family, and knew that his brother still planned to kill him. He thought that he could pay his brother off with some livestock. But Esau refused to accept them as a gift and assembled four hundred men to go with him to kill Jacob and his family.

When Jacob discovered this, he was terrified. So he did what any sensible person would do. He asked God to intervene and help him see his brother in peace. Because Jacob was such a treacherous person, he was not sure whether God was going to help him.

The word came to Jacob that Esau and his army of four hundred men would be there the next day to annihilate him and his family.

That night Jacob prayed to the Lord. During the night, the Lord sent an angel to wrestle with Jacob. According to the Scriptures, Jacob wrestled with the angel all night. At daybreak, the angel begged Jacob to let him go. But Jacob told the angel: **"I won't let you go until you bless me."** According to the Scriptures, the angel blessed Jacob and changed him name to Israel.

According to the Scriptures, in spite of his situation—his brother planning to bring an army or four hundred men against him and not knowing if he was going to live or die—Jacob refused to give up on God.

The text says that Jacob wrestled with a man or an angel of the Lord. However, in actuality, Jacob was really wrestling with God Himself. God had come in the form of a man and wrestled with Jacob all night long.

That why Jacob was told, **"You have wrestled with God and with men and have overcome."**

Jacob was able to "overcome" because he refused to stop wrestling with God until God blessed him. Because of Jacob's situation, it should be obvious that the "blessing" he wanted from God was to be able to see his brother in peace. As a result of going to God in prayer and wrestling with God all night long, the next day, when Jacob met his brother, Esau **"ran to his brother, embraced him, and kissed him!"**

The lesson for us is: Regardless of the seriousness or hopelessness of your situation, don't give up on God.

Don't give up on God being able to intervene in your situation.
Don't give up on God being able to deal with your situation.
Don't give up on God being able to handle your situation.
Don't give up on God being able to correct your situation.
Don't give up on God being able to touch hearts.
Don't give up on God being able to change minds.
Don't give up on God being able to transform lives.
Don't give up on God being able to open doors.
Don't give up on God being able to "make a way out of no way!"

Sometimes your situation is bad, and God lets it get worse. Sometimes you may wonder **why** God lets your situation go from bad to worse and doesn't step in. Sometime you may wonder **why** God doesn't do something.

Sometimes I believe God looks at our situation and says: "If I step in now, they may not know that I did it. But if I let things get as bad as they can get then step in, they will know that I did it. They will know that this was not an accident. They will know that this did not happen because of their human ability. They will know that this was humanly impossible. They will know that a God had to be involved in this. They will know

DON'T GIVE UP

that only God could do this. They will know that only an Omnipotent God can do this. They will know that only an Omniscient God can do this. They will know that only an Omnipresent God can do this. They will know that only a holy God can do this."

If you're God's child you have been delivered from the kingdom of Satan to the Kingdom of God. If you're God's child, Satan wants to get you back into his kingdom and he will do everything he can to try to make you lose your faith and confidence in God. If you're God's child, Satan WANTS YOU to "give up on God!"

The story of Shadrach, Meshach, and Abednego is one of the most dramatic and moving examples of refusing to give up on God.

Their story covers all of chapter three in the Book of Daniel.

According to this chapter, the king ordered that at the sound of the music. At the sound of the horn. At the sound of the harp. At the sound of the flute. At the sound of the other musical instruments, ALL of those living in this province of Babylon were to STOP what they were doing to bow down and worship the ninety-foot golden image that the king had set up on the plain of Dura.

According to the Scriptures, *when* these three young men refused to bow down to the ninety-foot image of gold that King Nebuchadnezzar set up, he threatened to have them thrown into a burning fiery furnace. In Daniel 3:16-18, they told King Nebuchadnezzar:

"We do not need to defend ourselves in this matter. If we are thrown into the blazing furnace, the God whom we serve is *able* to deliver us. And he will deliver us from your hand. But, even if He does *NOT* deliver us, we want you to know, O king, that we will NOT serve your gods or worship the image of gold you have set up." (NIV)

145

As a result of refusing to give up on God, when they were thrown into a blazing fiery furnace that had been heated "seven times hotter" than it had ever been, THE LORD GOD DELIVERED THEM!

According to the Scriptures:

On Mt. Moriah, Abraham refused to give up on God. Even after laying his son, Isaac, on the alter and his son asking him where was the sacrifice, because he hadn't given up on God, Abraham told his son: **"God himself will provide the lamb for the burnt offering" (Gen. 22:8, NIV)**

According to the Scriptures:

In spite of being sold into slavery by his brother, Joseph refused to give up on God. Because Joseph refused to give up on God, God blessed him to prepare Egypt for the coming famine and to have enough food to share with other nations. and with his family. That's why Joseph could tell his brothers: **"You intended to harm me, but God intended it for good to accomplish what is now being done, the saving of many lives." (Gen. 50:20, NIV)**

According to the Scriptures:

After he lost his strength and his sight, Samson refused to give up on God. Because he refused to give up on God, God restored his strength and let Samson avenge his enemies.

According to the Scriptures:

In spite of his adversity, Job refused to give up on God. In spite of his children being killed, his health being taken, and his property being stolen, Job refused to give up on God. Instead of giving up on God, Job said, **"Though he slay me, yet will I hope in him." (Job 13:15, NIV)**

According to the Scriptures:

In spite of the death of her husband, and her mother-in-law urging her to go live with other members of her family, Ruth refused to give up on God. Because Ruth refused to give up on God, she was able to tell Naomi:

"Don't urge me to leave you or to turn back from you. Where you go, I will go and where you stay, I will stay. Your people will be my people and your God my God. Where you die, I will die, and there I will be buried." (Ruth 1:16-17, NIV)

According to the Scriptures:

Although she knew that her life was on the line for trusting God, Queen Esther refused to give up on God. Instead, she put her life on the line in order to save her people and said: **"If I perish, I perish!" (Esther 4:16, NIV)**

According to the Scriptures:

Even after being told by God's prophet that he was going to die, King Hezekiah refused to give up on God. Instead, he turned his face to the wall and prayed and **God added fifteen years to his life.** (2 Kings 20:6, NIV)

CONCLUSION

Regardless of what happens in your life, don't give up on God. Regardless of the situation, don't give up on God. Regardless of the circumstances, don't give up on God. Regardless of how you feel, don't give up on God. Regardless of how bad things get, don't give up on God.

Instead of giving **up** on God, give **over** to God. Instead of giving up on God, put it in God's hands. Instead of giving up on God, let God handle it.

Instead of giving up on God, stand on your faith. When you stand on your faith, you know that:

"In all things God works for the good of those who love him, who have been called according to his purpose." (Romans 8:28, NIV)

When you stand on your faith, you can say **"If God is for us, who can be against us?"** When you stand on your faith, you can say:

Who can separate us from the love of Christ? Shall trouble or hardship or persecution or famine or nakedness or danger or a sword? .... No, in all these things we are more than conquerors through him who loved us. For I am convinced that neither death nor life, neither angels nor demons, neither the present nor the future, nor any powers, neither height nor depth, nor anything else in all creation, will be able to separate us from the love of God that is in Christ Jesus our Lord. (Romans 8:35-39, NIV)

Regardless *of your situation.* **Regardless** *of the seriousness of your situation.* **Regardless** *of the hopelessness of your situation,* *DON'T GIVE UP ON GOD*

Don't give up on God being able to intervene in your situation.
Don't give up on God being able to deal with your situation.
Don't give up on God being able to handle your situation.
Don't give up on God being able to correct your situation.
Don't give up on God being able to touch hearts.
Don't give up on God being able to change minds.
Don't give up on God being able to transform lives.
Don't give up on God being able to open doors.
Don't give up on God being able to "make a way out of no way!"

WHATEVER happens to you. WHATEVER happens in your life. WHATEVER happens in your family. WHATEVER happens on your

DON'T GIVE UP

job. WHATEVER happens in your church. WHATEVER happens in your neighborhood. WHATEVER happens in your state. WHATEVER happens in your country. WHATEVER happens anywhere in the world: "DON'T GIVE UP ON GOD!"

QUESTIONS FOR REFLECTION & ACTION
After reading this sermon:

1. What did you learn from this sermon?
2. Have you ever thought of giving up on God?
3. If so, why did you think about doing so?
4. What do you think you need to know and do in order to never give up on God?

GOD FIRST

DON'T GIVE UP ON YOUR MARRIAGE
Matthew 19:1-6 (NIV)

INTRODUCTION

As we continue to look at God's Word for guidance and as we face and deal with personal and spiritual issues, let's continue the focus on the theme for this chapter: "Don't Give Up!"

The topic for this message will be
"Don't Give Up on Your Marriage!"

One of the struggles I had in preparing this series was to decide whether the message on "Don't Give Up on Your Marriage" should come before or come after the message on "Don't Give Up on Your Children."

Both marriage and children are a part of the institution of the family. The family, the institution of marriage, and children are under attack by the enemy.

It is evident from the actions of Satan in the Garden of Eden that he wants to destroy the family. In order to destroy the family, Satan seeks to destroy marriages.

Therefore, let's turn our attention to God's Word and see what God's Word has to say about marriage that can help married couples to know what they need to do in order to not give up on their marriage.

After Jesus told the parable of the unjust servant, Matthew 19:1-6 tells us that:

> *When Jesus had finished saying these things, He left Galilee and went into the region of Judea to the other side of the Jordan. Large crowds followed Him, and He healed them there. Some Pharisees came to Him to test Him. They asked, "Is it lawful for a man to divorce his wife for any and every reason?" Haven't you read," He replied, "that at the beginning the Creator made them male and*

150

DON'T GIVE UP

female," and said, "For this reason a man will leave his father and mother and be united to his wife, and the two will become one flesh." So they are no longer two but one. Therefore, what God has joined together, let man not separate. (NIV)

In this passage of Scripture, Jesus makes two main statements related to marriage.

The FIRST main statement is:
"A man shall leave his father and mother and be united to his wife"

Note: This instruction is given to the man—the husband. This verse says that when a man gets married, he is to "leave" his father and mother and "be united to" his wife. (The King James says, "cleave" to his wife).

Over the years, my wife and I have conducted many workshops and seminars and retreats for married couples. As a pastor, I have had the opportunity to counsel many couples—husbands and wives. One of the things that I have noticed is that some husbands and some wives have **not** "left" their father and mother.

SOME husbands are still tied too much to the parents. SOME wives are still tied too much to their parents.

SOME PARENTS contribute to this by telling their son or daughter "If it doesn't work out, you can always come back home!"

A "weak man" sees this statement by his parents as "a way out" of the marriage when the couple start having problems and difficulties—especially if he's a 'mama's boy." A "weak woman" sees this as "a way out" of the marriage when the couples start having problems and difficulties—especially if she's a "daddy's girl."

IF A COUPLE marries with the thought that either or both of them can "go back home" if things do go well for them, their marriage is DOOMED from the start.

151

IF A COUPLE doesn't take seriously the words "for better, for worse, for richer, for poorer, in sickness and in health, as long as we both shall live," it won't take much for one or both of them to want to end the marriage and go back home instead of doing everything they can reasonably do to WORK THINGS OUT!

MARRIAGE is a PARTNERSHIP. When PARTNERS are committed to their PARTNERSHIP, they know that there will be issues. They know there will be disagreements. They know there will need to be some compromises. They know they are going to have to make some sacrifices. Therefore, because they are committed to the partnership they are willing to do everything reasonable to WORK THINGS OUT!

The SECOND main statement is:
"What God has joined together, let no man separate."

This statement does not refer to a temporary separation but to divorce. Some couples need to "step back" for a while to "reassess" their marriage. This may involve a temporary separation. This can be a wise move. What Jesus is referring to here is not that kind of separation but to divorce.

Note: His hearers understood this. The reason why we know that His hearers understood this is because the PHARISEES asked him a question. Their question was not about separation, but about divorce.

When you read verses 7 through 14, the PHARISEES had a follow up question about MOSES allowing a man to give his wife a "certificate of divorce" and "sending her away." In response to this question, JESUS reminded them that Moses allowed them to do that "because of the hardness of their heart." JESUS also tells them that there is a legitimate reason for divorce: "marital unfaithfulness."

(Note: It's POSSIBLE for marital unfaithfulness to involve several things. BUT the only thing that thing that Jesus acknowledges specifically is ADULTERY. I may have to deal with that in another message).

DON'T GIVE UP

Whatever the case, divorce is here. Divorce is a fact of life and many couples get divorced every day.

According to recent statistics, Satan is being quite effective in destroying marriages. Recent statistics show that 50% of married couples end up getting divorced. Recent statistics also show that slightly more than 50% of married couples who say they are Christians end up getting a divorce.

I hope you picked up on that.

MORE couples who say they are Christians get divorced than couples who don't claim to be Christians. I wonder why? MY GUESS would be that it's possibly because Satan ATTACKS Christian couples MORE than he does other couples because he wants to get CHRISTIAN couples back in his kingdom. Satan already has the other couples in his kingdom.

In my teachings on spiritual warfare, I deal with "the strategies of Satan." Satan's strategies are so "successful" because few people—even few believers—are aware of them.

Notwithstanding the strategies of Satan, WHY do so many couples (especially Christian couples) get divorced? Obviously, there are many reasons. Let me list a few of them.

SOME COUPLES get divorced because of immaturity

Some couples get divorced because one or both of them is immature. One or both of them have not grown up and is childish. One or both of them insists on having their own way. Therefore, one or both of them is not ready for marriage.

SOME COUPLES get divorced because of infidelity

One of both of them have an affair. One or both of them is not really ready for marriage because one or both of them is not ready to be committed only to one another. One or both of them is not really ready to truly "settle down."

SOME COUPLES get divorced because of unrealistic expectations

One or both of them has unrealistic expectations. One or both of them expect everything to go well all the time. One or both of them expect to not have any problems. One or both of them expect more from each other than is realistic. This is another example of immaturity.

SOME COUPLES get divorced because they are unequally yoked

To be unequally yoked is to be married to the wrong person. It doesn't matter how much you think you "love" one another, if you marry the wrong person it's not going to work. In 2 Corinthians 6:14-16, the Apostle Paul says,

"Do not be unequally yoked with unbelievers. For what do righteousness and wickedness have in common? Or what fellowship can light have with darkness? What harmony is there between Christ and Belial? What does a believer have in common with an unbeliever? What agreement is there between the temple of God and idols? For we are the temple of the living God. As God has said, "I will live with them and walk among them, and I will be their God, and they will be My people."

SOME COUPLES get divorced because they marry for the wrong reason

Some people get married for the wrong reason. Some people get married because they want companionship. People who marry for companionship get married because they are lonely. Instead of getting married, these people need to get themselves a dog or a cat or something

DON'T GIVE UP

else to be their companion and keep them company. Some people get married for security. If you can't take care of yourself, you should not get married just to have someone to take care of you.

YES, there are many reasons why couples get divorced. According to statistics, most divorced couples say that problems in the area of sex or money was the main reason for their divorce. If a couple is having problems in either of these areas, it creates problems in other areas and make those problems look even bigger.

Among couples under thirty years old, 80% of them say that "money problems" was the main reason for their divorce.

YET, many couples stand before an official every day and say: "For better, for worse, for richer, for poorer, in sickness and in health, as long as we both shall live."

WHAT, then, can help married couples keep this commitment? WHAT can help them maximize their possibility for having a good marriage?

The KEY is found in the phrase:
"WHAT GOD HAS JOINED TOGETHER!"

If God joined you together, you can have a good marriage. If God did not join you together, you are in trouble.

MANY couples have not been joined together by God. SOME couples have been joined together by Satan. SOME couples have been joined together by "the flesh." So the key is for a couple to be joined together by God.

In order for a couple to be "joined together by God," they need to ASK God for guidance. They need to ASK God if this is His will. They need to WAIT for God's answer and DO what God says. They may even want to ask God for some specific "sign" that indicates that this is God's will for them.

155

BENNIE HINN learned the value of doing this. In one of his books, he reports that he was dating a young lady and felt in his heart that "she was the one." He wanted to ask her to marry him, but he decided to consult God first. When he did so, he decided to use the biblical concept of "the fleece." Simply, he decided to tell God that if His answer was "Yes," this young lady would do something that only he and God knew about.

Before leaving for a preaching engagement, this young lady drove him to the airport and promised to pick him up when he returned. He told God that when this young lady picked him up at the airport, if she told him that she had a surprise for him—that she had baked for him his favorite cake—he would know that God's answer was that it was His will for him to ask her to marry him.

When Bennie Hinn returned. This young lady picked him up at the airport. She told him that she had a surprise for him. The "surprise" was that she had baked his favorite cake for him.

Everybody doesn't believe in using a "fleece." Even if you don't feel comfortable using a fleece, ASK God to "confirm" His answer in some way that you really know that He did it.

THE KEY to any couple having a happy marriage is for them to marry the right person. The only way to really know whether someone is "the right person" is to consult God. IF you earnestly and sincerely seek God. IF you earnestly and sincerely WANT to know God's will, He WILL reveal His will to you.

This statement is based on God's Word. This statement is based on God's Word that says:

> *"Trust in the Lord with all thine heart.*
> *Lean not to thy own understanding.*
> *In ALL thy ways acknowledge HIM and HE will*
> *DIRECT thy paths." (Prov. 3:5-6)*

DON'T GIVE UP

IF you marry the right person, YOU will have access to all of God's resources to help you have a good and happy marriage.

EVEN if you marry the right person, you WILL have some challenges. SATAN will see to that. BUT if you both trust and obey God, HE will help you *"resist the devil and he will flee from you." (James 4:7, NIV)*

Therefore, when challenges come,
DON'T GIVE UP ON YOUR MARRIAGE!

When Satan attacks it,
DON'T GIVE UP ON YOUR MARRIGGE!

When Satan attacks your marriage,
GO TO THE LORD IN PRAYER!

When you go to the Lord in prayer,
THE LORD WILL STRENTHEN YOU
AND YOUR MARRIAGE!

QUESTIONS FOR REFLECTION & ACTION
After reading this sermon:

1. What did you learn from this sermon?
2. What are some of the difficult issues in your marriage?
3. Why are they issues and what are you and your spouse doing about them?
4. What can, should, and will you and your spouse start doing about these issues?

DON'T GIVE UP ON YOUR CHILDREN
Matthew 15:22-28 (NIV)

INTRODUCTION

Does this text look familiar? It should, because in our series of sermons on "Help for The Christian Home" it was the text for our message on "Help for Christian Mothers." Although it is the same text and although the first part of this message will look at some of the points made in that sermon, as you will soon see, this is definitely not the same sermon but a different sermon on the present theme: "DON'T GIVE UP."

In the previous messages on this theme, you were encouraged to "Don't Give Up on God" and "Don't Give Up on Your Marriage." In this message you will be encouraged to "Don't Give Up on Your Children."

Being a parent in not easy. Being a parent has its ups and downs. Being a parent has its trials and tribulations. Being a parent has its joys and sorrows.

Sometimes parents feel like giving up. Sometimes, parents feel like giving up on their children. Sometimes parents feel like giving up on their sons. Sometimes parents feel like giving up on their daughters.

In fact, some parents really **do** give up on their children. Some parents actually **do** give up on their sons. Some parents actually **do** give up on their daughters.

After so many ups and downs. broken promises and disappointments, some parents actually do give up on their children.

In spite of those things, as loving parents, we should do everything we can to **not** give up on our children.

In this message, I would like to introduce you to a mother who **refused** to give up on her daughter.

OBSERVATION

After Jesus rebuked the Pharisees in Jerusalem, Matthew 15:22-28 tells us that:

DON'T GIVE UP

Leaving that place, Jesus withdrew to the region of Tyre and Sidon. A Canaanite woman from that vicinity came to Him, crying out, "Lord, Son of David, have mercy on me! My daughter is suffering terribly from demon-" possession" Jesus did not answer her a word. So His disciples came to Him and urged Him, "Send her away, for She keeps crying after us." Her answered, "I was sent only to the lost sheep of Israel."

The woman came and knelt before Him. "Lord, help me!" she said. He replied, "It is not right to take the children's bread and toss it to their dogs." "Yes, Lord," she said "but even the dogs eat the crumbs that fall from their master's table." Then Jesus answered, "Woman, you have great faith! Your request is granted." And her daughter was healed from that very hour.

According to this passage of Scripture, there are **four** basic things that this mother did that helped her daughter.

According to these verses:
This mother knew that her daughter had a problem.

This mother knew that her daughter was sick. This mother knew that her daughter needed help.

As parents, we should *know* when our children are sick and need help. As parents, we should *know* when our children need help. As parents, we should *know* when our children have a problem. As parents, we should *know* our children well enough to know when they need help.

As parents, we should *know* when our children have a physical, spiritual, or emotional problem. As parents, we should *know* when our children have a drug problem.

159

According to these verses:
This mother saw her daughter's problem as her problem

According to our text, this mother saw her daughter's problem as her problem. Look at what she said: *"Lord, help ME because my daughter is suffering terribly from demon-possession."*

This mother told Jesus that she needed help because her daughter needed help.

As parents, we need to realize that when our children have a problem, *we* have a problem. If **one** person in the family has a problem, the whole family has a problem because that person's problem *affects* the **whole** family. This woman saw her daughter's problem as her problem.

If your child has a drug problem, every member of your family has a problem **believing** and **trusting** that person. As parents, we need to see our children's problem as our problem.

According to these verses:
This mother believed that her daughter could be helped

According to these verses, this mother **believed** that her daughter could be helped. That's why she went to Jesus. This mother went to Jesus because she **believed** that Jesus could help her. That's why she said, "Lord, help me!"

Regardless of the problem. Regardless of the need. Regardless of the situation. Regardless of the sickness. Regardless of the addiction. We need to **believe** that our child **can** be helped. We have to continue to **believe** that our child can be helped.

WHY? Because when we **stop believing** that our child can be helped, we **stop seeking** help for that child. When we **stop seeking** help for our child, that child is doomed!

DON'T GIVE UP

According to these verses:
This mother got help for her daughter

According to these verses, this mother got help for her daughter. **Even** when Jesus ignored her. **Even** when Jesus insulted her by calling her a dog. **Even** when His disciples wanted to send her away, this mother got down on her knees and begged Jesus to **help** her daughter.

This mother *knew* that her daughter needed help and she was *determined* to get help for her daughter. Because this mother was *determined* to get help for her daughter, she *refused* to give up. Because this mother was *determined* to get help for her daughter, she *refused* to give up on her daughter. Because this mother was *determined* to bet help for her daughter, she *refused* to be stopped. This mother got help for her daughter. According to the Scripture, because of this mother's faith, **"her daughter was healed from that very hour."**

Fortunately, this mother also **knew** where to get help. Unfortunately, many parents today **don't know** where to go when their children need help—**especially** when they have a spiritual problem. Although problems may manifest themselves physically or emotionally, many of them have a spiritual root.

In order to help you to understand this, let's look at a mother who had a son with some serious problems but she refused to give up on him. Because this mother knew that her son's problem was basically spiritual, she went to the Lord for help. Hopefully, each of us can learn from what she did and be willing to seek the Lord's help.

THE STORY OF MONICA

The story of Monica and her love for her family is one of the greatest stories of a mother who refused to give up on her children.

Monica was the wife of an abusive, pagan husband who had a violent temper. She married her husband because her parents (who were

Christians) wanted her to do so. In this abusive marriage, Monica had three children.

Although her husband was a pagan (an unbeliever), he allowed her try to raise her children to be Christians.

One of her children, Augustine, was a free-spirited young man who did everything he was big enough to do. He did drugs. He consumed alcohol in great quantities. He was "a player." He was a "ladies man." He had a reputation for being **very** sexually promiscuous. He had a **child** by one of his sexual partners and they lived together for a while. Augustine had a very **bad** reputation.

In spite of all this, his mother, Monica, prayed **fervently** for his salvation. She prayed **fervently** for her husband's salvation. She prayed **fervently** for the salvation of her other children—but especially for Augustine **because** he was the wildest. HE was the most depraved and unruliest. HE was the most disrespectful. Augustine, was the one who truly broke her heart the most.

Nevertheless, Monica **continued** to pray for him. Monica **continued** to ask God to save him. Monica **continued** to ask others to pray for him. Monica **continued** to ask others to pray for him to be delivered from sexual promiscuity and drug abuse.

Monica continued to do this during most of his early life. Augustine lived a fast life and did his own thing. Augustine **did** whatever he wanted to do, **to** whoever he wanted to do it to, and **didn't care** what anybody thought about it—**including** his mother, Monica.

THEN one day, when Augustine was about 32 years old, her prayers were answered. After all of those years, Augustine finally accepted Jesus Christ as his Lord and Savior. After all of those years, Augustine finally got saved. After all of those years, Augustine finally got delivered. After all of those years, Augustine finally got delivered from drugs. After all of those years, Augustine finally got delivered from alcohol. After all of those years, Augustine finally got delivered from sexual promiscuity.

DON'T GIVE UP

THAT was just the beginning.

AFTER Augustine got saved, baptized, and confirmed, Augustine became a **priest**.

AFTER he became a **priest**, Augustine became a **bishop**—the Bishop of Hippo in North Africa.

AFTER he became a **bishop**, he became one of the **greatest theologians** in the Christian church.

These things didn't happen by accident. These things happened because a mother refused to give up on her son. These things happened because a mother refused to stop praying for her son. These things happened because a mother refused to stop praying for her son's salvation, and deliverance from drugs, alcohol, and sexual promiscuity.

As a result of her prayers. As a result of Monica's prayers. Not only did her son get saved, but her HUSBAND also got saved. Her abusive and violent husband, ALSO got saved.

WHEN he got saved, he said that what caused him to accept Christ was HIS WIFE'S FAITH. HIS WIFE'S PRAYERS. HIS WIFE'S KINDNESS—IN SPITE OF HIS MEANNESS!

As a result of her devotion and dedication to her family. As a result of Monica's continued fervent prayers for her family. The Roman Catholic church has made her

THE PATRON SAINT OF MOTHERS AND WIVES

CONCLUSION

PARENTS, don't give up on your children.

MOTHERS, don't give up on your children.

FATHERS, don't give up on your children.

Instead of "giving up" on your children, "give them over" to JESUS. Give them "over" to the LORD.

GOD FIRST

WHATEVER the problem Whatever the need. WHATEVER the situation. WHATEVER the manifestation, you can take your child to JESUS. You can take your child's problem to JESUS. When your child has a problem, take it to the Lord in prayer. When your child has a physical problem, take it to the Lord in prayer. When your child has a spiritual problem, take it to the Lord in prayer. When your child has an emotional problem, take it to the Lord in prayer. When your child has a drug problem, take it to the Lord in prayer. When your child has an alcohol problem, take it to the Lord in prayer. When your child has an attitude problem take it to the Lord in prayer.

WHY? Because Jesus said,

"ASK and it will be given to you. SEEK and you will find. KNOCK and the door shall be opened to you." (Matt. 7:7, NIV)

When you, your child, or your family have a problem, "Take it to the Lord in prayer!"

When you take it to the Lord in prayer, "ASK the Savior to help you. COMFORT, strengthen and keep you. HE is able to help you. HE will carry you through!" (The New National Baptist Hymnal, Triad Publications, 1977)

WHEN you take it to the Lord is prayer: P.U.S.H—Pray Until Something Happens!

DON'T GIVE UP

QUESTIONS FOR REFLECTION & ACTION
After reading this sermon:

1. What did you learn from this sermon?
2. What are some of the reasons why some parents give up on their children?
3. Have you thought of giving up on any of your children? If so, why?
4. What kept you from giving up on your children and what do you need to learn and do to not give up on them?

GOD FIRST

DON'T GIVE UP ON YOURSELF
Psalm 51:1-10 (NIV)

INTRODUCTION

In this final sermon on the theme **"Don't Give Up,"** we're going to get a bit more personal and focus our attention on the topic: **"Don't Give Up on Yourself."**

All of us make mistakes. Sometimes, we make the same mistake over and over again. At some time, all of us have determined to break a specific habit. Some of us have been trying to break some habit for several years. Some of us have been trying to break some habit since our youth or over many years.

Some of us have been trying for so long that we've given up. Some people have given up on breaking some habit or avoiding some mistake. Some people are so disappointed in themselves that they have decided to give up on themselves and their hopes and dreams.

Regardless of how many times you have tried and failed, it's dangerous to give up on yourself. Regardless of how many times you have "messed up," it's dangerous to give up on yourself.

People who give up on themselves often become alcoholics. People who give up on themselves often become drug addicts. Some people who give up on themselves commit suicide. Some people who give up on themselves often engage in some form of self-destructive behavior.

It's dangerous to give up on yourself. It's dangerous to give up. Therefore, I want to encourage you to never, ever, never give up on yourself.

OBSERVATION

As I seek to encourage you to never give up on yourself, let's look at someone who messed up big time. Let's look at someone who failed God and himself. Let's look at someone who failed himself. Let's look

166

DON'T GIVE UP

at someone who committed "big time sins" and could have given up on himself. But, by the grace of God he didn't give up on himself.

That person was King David. David messed up big time and jeopardized his relationship with God and his family.

Let's turn our attention to Psalm 51:1-13 to see what David did and see how, in spite of it all, David refused to give up on himself.

In this psalm David cries out:

Have mercy on me, O God, according to your unfailing love, according to your great compassion, blot out my transgressions. Wash away all my iniquity and cleanse me of my sin. For I know my transgressions, and my sin is always before me. Against You, You only, have I sinned and done what is evil in Your sight, so that you are proved right when You speak and justified when You judge. Surely, I was sinful at birth, sinful from the time my mother conceived me. Surely you desire truth in the inner parts, You teach me wisdom in the innermost place. Cleanse me with hyssop, and I will be clean; wash me, and I will be whiter than snow. Let me hear joy and gladness, let the bones You have crushed rejoice. Hide Your face from my sins and blot out all my iniquity. Create in me a pure hear, O God, and renew a steadfast spirit within me. Do not cast me from Your presence or take Your Holy Spirit from me. Restore to me the joy of Your salvation and grant me a willing spirit to sustain me. Then will I teach transgressors Your ways, and sinners will turn back to You. (NIV)

In this Scripture, David was remembering his sins. In this Scripture, David was remembering that after he got Bathsheba pregnant (who was married to his soldier, Uriah), he tried to cover it up by giving her husband a furlough from his military duties to come home and be with his wife. He would then (hopefully) have intercourse with her and get her pregnant so that he would think that the baby was his.

167

GOD FIRST

According to the Scriptures, Uriah took the overnight furlough but refused to go in to have sex with his wife, because he felt it was unfair for him to do so when his fellow soldiers did not have that opportunity.

When David discovered that Uriah did not have sex with his wife, he ordered the captain of his troops to put Uriah in the front line the next day when the army went into battle. David gave orders to the captain to wait until the battle got heavy, and if Uriah had not been killed, to order his troops to pull back and leave Uriah out in front by himself so that he would surely be killed. They did so, and Uriah died in battle

In this Scripture, David was remembering his sin of adultery. In this Scripture, David was remembering his orders to the captain of his army that made sure that Uriah would be killed in battle. This made David not only guilty of murder but also of making the captain and the soldiers be his unknowing accomplices.

As David remembered all of this, he became angry with himself. David was disappointed in himself. David was disgusted with himself.

Because of how he felt about himself, his actions, and his behavior, David could have "given up" on himself. But by the grace of God, instead of "giving up" on himself, David repented of all of his sins!

Instead of giving up on himself, David asked the Lord to have mercy on him, blot out his transgressions, and forgive him. for all of his sins. Instead of giving up on himself, David asked the Lord to create in him a clean heart, renew a right spirit within him, and restore to him the joy of his salvation. Instead of giving up on himself, David promised to help other sinners come back to Him.

When you study the life of David, you will discover that, in spite of his sins, faults, failures, mistakes. weaknesses, and shortcomings, BECAUSE **he repented** of his sins and asked God to make him a new and better person, **God GRANTED his request!**

There's a lesson in this for us. There's a lesson in this for us today. There's a lesson in this for you and me. There's a lesson in this for every

DON'T GIVE UP

person on the face of the earth.

That lesson is:

IN SPITE OF your weaknesses, don't give up on yourself.

IN SPITE OF your sins, don't give up on yourself.

IN SPITE OF your shortcomings, don't give up on yourself.

IN SPITE OF faults, don't give up on yourself.

IN SPITE OF failures, don't give up on yourself

IN SPITE OF imperfections, don't give up on yourself.

The lesson for you today is:

INSTEAD OF giving up on yourself, ask the Lord to have mercy and forgive you. INSTEAD OF giving up on yourself, ask the Lord to cleanse you. INSTEAD OF giving up on yourself, ask the Lord cleanse you, create in you a clean heart. renew the right spirit within you, and restore the joy of your salvation.

AFTER you ask the Lord to fix you, YOU need to promise the Lord that you will teach transgressors His ways.

AFTER you ask the Lord to fix you, YOU need to promise to help sinners come to Him.

AFTER you ask the Lord to fix you, YOU need to promise to help sinners accept Jesus Christ as their Lord and Savior.

AFTER you ask the Lord to fix you, YOU need to promise to encourage and help other believers to remain true to the faith.

CONCLUSION

Somebody reading this may be asking:

HOW can I help sinners to be saved?

HOW can I help backsliders to come back to Christ?

HOW can I help other believers to remain true to the faith?

In order to help sinners to get saved, you need to begin by PRAYING for their salvation. You need to **"Talk to God about them before you talk to them about God!"** so that God can prepare them and prepare you. So that God will tell you when to do deeds of kindness for them and when to plant seeds of salvation that He can use to help them become disciples of Jesus Christ and disciple-makers for Jesus Christ.

WHEN the Lord leads you to do so, you need to tell them how to get saved. You need to share with them the ABC's of Salvation.

The A of Salvation is:
"ALL have sinned and come short of the glory of God."
(Romans 3:23, NIV)

The B of Salvation is:
"BELIEVE on the Lord Jesus Christ and you will be saved."
(Acts 16:31, NIV)

The C of Salvation is:
"If you CONFESS with your mouth that Jesus is Lord and believe in your heart that God raised him from the dead, and you will be saved."
(Romans 10:9-10, NIV)

In order to help fellow believers to continue to grow in the faith, you need to remind them to read their Bible and pray every day. You need to remind and encourage them be faithful and consistent in worshiping and serving God by discovering and using their spiritual gifts to glorify God, to edify His Church, and to advance His Kingdom

Encourage them to read the second. chapter in the Book of Acts about the coming of the Holy Spirit and "the birth of the church."

DON'T GIVE UP

Encourage them to read Hebrews 10:22-25 about the importance of worshiping God with other believers.

Encourage them to buy a Bible version they can understand, with a good commentary, and read passages telling them what Christians should do for one another.

Then ASK THE HOLY SPIRIT what else He wants you to do to help them remain true to the faith.

QUESTIONS FOR REFLECTION & ACTION

AFTER READING THIS SERMON:

1. What did you learn from this sermon?
2. Are you having difficulty forgiving yourself for anything? If so, what?
3. Why has it been difficult to forgive yourself for this?
4. What can, should and will you do to forgive yourself and move forward?

GOD FIRST

CHAPTER FIVE

WHAT DO THESE STONES MEAN?

"What Do These Stones Mean?"
(Part One)
"What Do These Stones Mean?"
(Part Two)
"What Do These Stones Mean?"
(Part Three)
"What Do These Stones Mean?"
(Part Four)

WHAT DO THESE STONES MEAN?
Joshua 4:1-7 (NIV) (Part One)

INTRODUCTION

According to Joshua 4:1-7, the Lord God delivered the children of Israel from 430 years of slavery in Egypt. After He enabled them to cross the Red Sea on dry ground and as they entered the Promised Land, the Lord God enabled them to also cross the Jordan River on dry ground.

According to these verses, when the whole nation of Israel finished crossing the Jordan, the Lord God told Joshua to choose one man from each of the twelve tribes of Israel and have each of them to pick up a stone in the river and carry it to the other side. The Lord God told Joshua that these stones would serve as memorial of what the Lord had done so that, in days to come, when their children and grand-children see this memorial and ask the question: *"What do these stones mean?"* they would be told that these stones are a reminder that the Lord God stopped the flow of the river so that the ark of the covenant could be carried across on dry ground.

OBSERVATION

Each year during the month of February, African Americans recognize and celebrate the journey of African Americans. A journey that started in Africa and went from slavery to freedom. A journey that went from segregation to emancipation.

In this series of sermons, we will look at some significant aspects of that journey and look at some of the significant people (black and white, men and women) who helped us on this journey. In these sermons, we will look at several significant "stones" that played a significant role in our journey. We begin this series by looking at our "Heritage Stone" and our "Millstones."

HERITAGE STONE

The heritage stone is the stone that reminds us that Africa is the cradle of civilization. The heritage stone reminds us that the beginnings of the human race can be traced back to "Mother Africa." Consequently, Africa is not only the origin of Black Americans but of the human race. Therefore, not only Black Americans but the whole human race should realize and celebrate that we had our origin on the continent of Africa.

People in general, Black Americans, especially, should never forget our African heritage. Black Americans should never forget that our ancestors were African kings and queens. Black Americans should never

WHAT DO THESE STONES MEAN?

forget that our ancestors were the first physicians, first scientists, first mathematicians, and first astronomers.

Black Americans should never forget that although we were born in this country our roots go back to "Mother Africa."

THE MILLSTONE OF SLAVERY

Slavery was the first millstone that African Americans had to endure. People around the world, but especially Black Americans, should never forget the millstone of slavery.

The African slave trade began in 1442. It began with the Portuguese and quickly spread all over the continent of Europe.

In the 1600s, long before the United States became a country in 1776, many people in the thirteen colonies and other areas joined and became prominent participants in the African slave trade. Although slavery was most prominent in the South, it also existed in the North to a significant extent.

Slavery was exceedingly profitable. Because slave labor was free, the primary expense that slave-owners had was the expense to transport potential slaves from Africa and maintaining them after they arrived.

In order to maximize their potential profit from selling Black Africans into slavery, those doing the transporting packed as many people as possible (men, women, and children) on their ship. Some of them were known as "loose packers" and others were known as "tight packers" (they packed more than the loose packers).

These potential slaves traveled under horrid conditions.

In addition to being separated from people from the same area so they would not be able to communicate with each other, men and women, boys and girls were chained together for the long journey and were unchained for only about an hour a day. They were hosed down daily and given just enough to eat to keep them alive. Many died from disease. Some committed suicide by jumping overboard.

175

GOD FIRST

In order to free their children from such horrid conditions, some mothers threw their children overboard.

For some two hundred years, sharks followed these slave ships for hundreds of miles in order to feed on dead corpses or live people who jumped overboard or threw their children overboard.

The African slave trade was a millstone. It was the first millstone that these captured, kidnapped, or purchased people had to endure.

Because slaves were legal property, their owners could do whatever they wanted to do to them. Raping young girls and women and castrating men was very prevalent.

Post-Civil War Slavery

Although the 13th Amendment to the Constitution officially abolished slavery, white businessmen and politicians found ways to get around this amendment.

States like Alabama and South Caroline passed laws known as "Black Codes," which gave officials the right to arrest Black people for almost any reason and force them to work for their release if they were unable to pay the fine. Since they were almost always unable to pay their fine, they had to do manual labor for a specific period of time.

Almost every southern state had some form of what was known as the "Convict Lease System," which allowed Blacks to be charged for almost anything that the state or county considered a crime for Blacks and lease them to local and to out-of-state businesses and industries who paid the state for the labor that these "convicts" provided.

During the years after the Civil War known as the period of Reconstruction, more than 200,000 black people were subjected to this kind of treatment. Many were chained, beaten, flogged, and sexually violated. Thousands died from injuries, disease, and torture. Most were charged with petty "crimes" such as vagrancy.

This system was later replaced with another repressive system known as "the chain gang."

WHAT DO THESE STONES MEAN?

Michelle Alexander describes the convict release system in her book, *The New Jim Crow*. W.E.B. DuBois said that during this period "the slave went free; stood a brief moment in the sun; then back again toward slavery."[11]

The Millstone of Segregation

Those who survived the journey from Africa to the United States and were sold into slavery had yet another millstone to endure. It was the millstone of segregation.

Segregation replaced the African slave trade as a millstone. Segregation made African Americans second-class citizens. Under segregation, a law was passed that said Black Americans were only 3/5 of a person.

Segregation limited Black Americans. Segregation was the apartheid of the South that passed laws to keep Blacks and whites apart as much as possible and to make sure that Blacks knew that, at best, they were second-class citizens.

I grew up in the South in the 1940s. I recall having to ride in the back of the bus. I recall having to give up my seat at the back of the bus to a white person to keep them from having to stand. I recall having to observe that some drinking fountains were for Blacks and others were for Whites. Those for Blacks were always of less quality and often didn't work.

Some communities had laws that said a black person must get off the sidewalk to let a white person pass. Blacks were expected to look down when talking to a white person and to always say "Yes, Ma'am and "No Ma'am" or "Yes, Sir" and "No, Sir."

Under segregation, black people of all ages were expected to refer to little white girls as "Miss." This was depicted quite vividly in the Shirley Temple movies when she was only about six years old and black children and adults referred to her as "Miss Shirley."

---

11   Michelle Alexander, The New Jim Crow: Mass Incarceration in the Age of Colorblindness (New York: New Press, 2020).

GOD FIRST

When Blacks went to the movies, they had to sit in the balcony. If there was no room for white people to sit downstairs, they could come to the balcony and Blacks people would have to give up their seat.

Some facilities in the South did not cater to Blacks at all. The facilities that did were always segregated. Blacks could not enter the same door as whites. They had to go to the back door. Blacks could not sit in the same area as whites. There was a separate area for them.

Almost everything in the South was segregated. Some things, like swimming pools, were not open to Blacks at all. Churches were segregated. There were segregated facilities on trains and buses. Schools were not only segregated but black schools had inferior facilities, used books, and limited resources.

These conditions prompted black and white students from the North and from the South to go to some of these facilities and engage in peaceful protests known as "Sit-Ins" and "Wade-Ins."

There were county and state fairs all over the South. Primarily for economic reasons, Blacks were able to go on certain days. These days were known as "Negro Day." These were the only days that Blacks could go, but whites could go on any day. Only a few whites went on **"Negro Day."**

In order to know where you could go and not go in the South, (especially when you were traveling) Blacks produced what were called **"Green Books."** These books let you know what accommodations were available and not available to you if you were black. So, before you got on the road, you would know where you could buy gas, get food, or use the restroom that would be clearly marked "Colored."

Because of these "Jim Crow" laws of segregation, there were almost no hotels in the South available to Blacks. Blacks who traveled had to stay with friends or relatives or sleep in their car.

In 1964, Margaret and I had to sleep in our car because there were no hotel accommodations for Blacks in the area of Texas we were passing through.

WHAT DO THESE STONES MEAN?

One of the most sinister things that segregation tried to do was to make Blacks hate or despise their blackness. Fair-skinned Blacks were treated better and often told that they were better than Blacks who were darker. Unfortunately, some Blacks bought in to this.

Some black churches (especially in the South) made sure that lighter skinned Blacks sat on one side of the church and darker skinned Blacks sat on the other.

Blacks who bought into this kind of thinking
would say to each other:

"If you're white, you're all right.
If you're brown, stick around.
If you're black, get back."

However, most Blacks did not buy into this and fought this kind
of thinking with saying like:

"The blacker the berry, the sweeter the juice."

During the Black Power movement in the 1960s black people of
all ages would be heard saying:

"Say it loud. I'm black and I'm proud.
Say it loud. I'm black and I'm proud!"

CONCLUSION

By the grace of God, Black Americans have come a long way. We have come from slavery to emancipation. We have come from segregation to integration. But we still have a long way to go.

GOD FIRST

These stones remind us of the goodness and grace of God. These stones remind us that God is the God of love, mercy and compassion. These stones remind us that God is the God of freedom, and liberation.

QUESTIONS FOR REFLECTION & ACTION
After reading this sermon:

1. What did you learn about the heritage stone and the millstones of slavery and segregation?
2. How did learning (or being reminded of this) make you feel?
3. What troubles (concerns) you most about these stones?
4. What more would you like to learn about these stones?
5. What millstones still need to be moved?
6. What are you willing to do to help identify and remove them?

WHAT DO THESE STONES MEAN?
Joshua 4:1-7 (NIV) (Part Two)

INTRODUCTION

In our last sermon, we looked at The Heritage Stone based upon our African heritage and the Millstones of Slavery and Segregation that African Americans had to endure in this country.

As we continue this series of sermons on "What Do These Stones Mean?" let's turn our attention to two other significant stones in the African American experience. Stones of Protest and Tombstones.

Stones of Protest

Contrary to some erroneous depictions of Black slaves as happy and content with their situation, the fact is that there were many forms of slave protests and even insurrections.

In Alex Haley's series, *Roots*, there was a scene where a house slave who was responsible for preparing meals for her owners spit into the food she was preparing. This is said to have not been uncommon. In some accounts of slave protests, some slaves ground up glass and put it in the food they were preparing for their master and his family. Some slaves ran away from the plantation and headed North. Some made it. Many did not make it and were captured, returned to the plantation, beaten, and maimed. Some were castrated.

I started school in Kemp, Texas. It was a segregated school. The textbooks that we used depicted slaves as happy. Slaves were shown singing and dancing. These textbooks were intended to give the impression that Black people enjoyed being slaves.

None of the textbooks that we read at that time recorded any slave protests nor slave rebellions. These textbooks did not tell of slaves who attempted to run away to freedom or committed suicide. These textbooks did not talk about Harriet Tubman and the underground railroad. These textbooks did not talk about northern abolitionists. These textbooks did not talk about Fredrick Douglass and his denunciation of our Fourth of July celebrations as a sham and as the apex of hypocrisy. These textbooks did not tell us about W.E.B. Dubois, Mary White Ovington, and the Niagara Movement that produced the N.A.A.C.P.—the National Association for the Advancement of Colored People.

These textbooks did tell us about the contributions of George Washington Carver and Booker T. Washington. We appreciated learning about Carver and his great scientific contributions in discovering hundreds of practical uses for the peanut and about Washington as a great educator who founded Tuskegee Institute that educated many Blacks during his day and has educated thousands since his time.

However, these books did not talk about Stones of Protest. Protests against slavery and segregation that involved Black and White men and women of conscience and integrity.

Some Protest Stones Were Verbal

Some of these stones of protest were verbal. White abolitionists like Wendell Phillips and William Lloyd Garrison spoke and wrote against slavery and tried to get legislation passed to abolish it. Black men and women like Frederick Douglass, Richard Allen, Henry Highland Garnet, and Sojourner Truth spoke out against and wrote articles against slavery and petitioned congress with pleas to abolish slavery.

Sojourner Truth was born Isabella Baumfree. She was born in slavery and escaped to freedom. She changed her name to Sojourner Truth after receiving a vision from the Lord telling her that she was to travel and spread the truth of God's love for all people of His will that men and women, Blacks and whites enjoy freedom, equality, and dignity.

The day she received this vision, she quit her job as a domestic and left her employer. Her employer advised her against doing this, but to no avail—she was convinced that this is what the Lord was telling her to do.

This stately black woman began her travels and spoke at many rallies and conventions on the abolition of slavery and on women's rights. The more she spoke the more she was in demand as a speaker. Consequently, she traveled and spoke in many Northern cities and states.

Her most famous speech, "Ain't I a Woman?" was given extemporaneously at a Women's Rights Convention in Ohio in 1851. This speech is one of the most famous speeches given on the abolition of slavery and on women's rights.

Her influence caught the attention of President Abraham Lincoln who met with her and give her the opportunity to present her case on the issue of abolishing slavery.

Another black woman who did much to aid slaves was Harriet Tubman. She was also born into slavery and ran away to freedom. She dedicated her life to helping other slaves to run away to freedom.

Harriet Tubman made nineteen trips to plantations in the South and brought some 300 slaves to freedom in the North. As the conductor of the Underground Railroad, she is regarded as "the Moses of her people." Although she could not read nor write she was smart and had great instincts and a great memory.

Harriet Tubman also served as a scout, a spy, a guerilla soldier, and as a nurse for the Union Army and provided medical care and treatment for both union and confederate soldiers. After the Civil War, she dedicated herself to helping impoverished former slaves in their transition from slavery to freedom.

Some Protest Stones Were Violent

Some protest stones were violent. The revolt of John Brown and his tiny army of black and white men (with some women as lookouts) was violent and led to the death of many—including John Brown and his sons.

The revolt led by Nat Turner (a black preacher) and his small army of black men was violent. They went from plantation to plantation during the night and killed white families as they lay in bed.

GOD FIRST

There were hundreds of slave revolts on plantations throughout the South that resulted in the death of many slave owners and their families. These revolts struck fear in white slave owners and their families throughout the South. Nat Turner's little army was killed, and he was captured, tortured, and hanged. His body was mutilated and parts of his body were sold as souvenirs.

Stones of Protest During Segregation

After slavery was legally abolished, stones of protest continued during segregation. Some of these stones of protest were verbal and involved speeches, letters of protest, and large demonstrations.

Most of these protests were acts of "civil disobedience." The sit-ins at lunch counters, the sit-ins at churches and on buses, and the wade-ins at swimming pools were all acts of civil disobedience that resulted in many people (Blacks and whites) being beaten and jailed.

Rosa Parks is known as "the mother of the civil rights movement," because she protested against the Alabama law that said that a black person had to give up his or her seat on the bus if a white person was standing. Rosa Parks was a seamstress who had worked all day and was on her way home. She had probably spent a good deal of time on her feet and was glad to be able to sit down on the bus. But when she refused to give up her seat to a white passenger, she was arrested.

Her act of civil disobedience triggered a bus boycott in the city of Montgomery that lasted over a year. During that time, the young pastor of the Dexter Avenue Baptist Church, The Rev. Dr. Martin Luther King, Jr., came into prominence and helped organize the Montgomery Improvement Association that promoted the boycott until the city decided to allow Blacks to sit anywhere on the buses and keep their seat, even if a white person was standing.

When the boycott ended, the bus company was almost bankrupt, because it had almost no black passengers. Even after the boycott

WHAT DO THESE STONES MEAN?

ended, the city bus company struggled because of a significant loss in ridership.

The Montgomery Improvement Association was a forerunner of the Southern Christian Leadership Council that was organized by King and other ministers to address the issue of segregation throughout the South. The SCLC conducted marches, sit-ins and other demonstrations throughout the South.

Many young people (black and white) participated in the marches and other demonstrations of both the SCLC and SCC. However, the Freedom Rides were sponsored and conducted primarily by SNCC and their participants were almost entirely black and white students from Northern and Southern colleges and universities.

Hundreds of black and white students from colleges and universities in the South and in the North rode buses across state lines and refused to observe the laws of segregation. Consequently, many of them were beaten and jailed for their actions.

The infamous "Bloody Sunday" experience on the First Sunday in March 1958, included black and white men, women and youth who marched from Selma, Alabama, and were stopped by violent state troopers at the Edmund Pettus Bridge. On that Sunday, hundreds of peaceful protesters were badly beaten. Among the many people who were badly beaten on "Bloody Sunday" was a young man named John Lewis, who was later elected to represent his congressional district in the state of Georgia. He has been re-elected in every election since that time and has served effectively and with distinction.

These and other acts of protest led to the adjudication of civil rights cases and the passage of significant civil rights legislation.

Many black students were not satisfied with the perceived "moderate" approach to the issue of segregation espoused by the Southern Christian Leadership Council and formed their own organization: The Student Non-Violent Coordinating Committee (SNCC).

185

GOD FIRST

Although SNCC was committed to non-violence, it was also committed to self-defense.

SNCC was initially led by Stokley Carmichael and H. Rap Brown. However, several men and women played a prominent role in the organization, growth, and development of this movement.

One of the most prominent players was a beautiful young black woman by the name of Diane Nash.

Diane was a key organizer and strategist. She led many sit-ins at lunch counters throughout the South. She was arrested several times. If she had been a man, she would have been as well-known other leaders of the movement.

Most people have not heard of Diane Nash. Most people don't know that she was one of the founders of SNCC—Student Nonviolent Coordinating Committee. Most people don't know that she organized and led many sit-ins. Most people don't know that she was a chief organizer of the "Freedom Rides."

Diane Nash was born into a Catholic family in Chicago in 1938. She was a beautiful baby and became a beautiful woman. She was beautiful enough to be the runner-up in an Illinois state beauty contest.

Diane Nash was not only beautiful, but she was smart and courageous. She was educated at Howard University in Washington D.C. and at Fisk University in Tennessee. She was one of the founders of SNCC and one of the organizers of Freedom Rides and sit-ins in several Southern states that included hundreds of Black and White students from throughout the country. She later married one of the most prominent Freedom Riders -- James Bevel. Diane Nash was about *seeking justice and correcting oppression.*

Because she was one of the leaders of many of many protests during the civil rights movement, she was beaten and jailed several times along with people like John Lewis and James Bevel.

WHAT DO THESE STONES MEAN?

In 1962, she was arrested in Jackson, Mississippi, and sentenced to two years in prison for teaching "non-violent tactics" to children and youth. At the time of her sentencing, she was four months pregnant.

Because of the outrage that was expressed throughout the North and the South, her sentence was reduced and she was released from prison. After her release from prison, she continued to play a major role in the civil rights movement throughout the South.

Later, she returned to Chicago and became an advocate for fair housing. In 2009, Fisk University awarded her an honorary degree.

Diana Nash was a freedom fighter, who dedicated her life to seeking justice and correcting oppression.

In order to eradicate the racial and social injustices in American society, an interracial civil rights organization was formed in 1909. That organization is known as the NAACP—the National Association for the Advancement of Colored People. Since 1909, the NAACP has been at the forefront in addressing racial and social injustices from a legal perspective.

Although many people (black and white) have played effective roles in the work of the NAACP, the man who stands head and shoulders above the rest is Thurgood Marshall.

Thurgood Marshall was born in Baltimore, Maryland, in 1908. His grandparents were slaves. His mother was an elementary school teacher. His father was a waiter. His parents put much emphasis on education and learning to think. His parents encouraged him and his siblings to solve puzzles, to engage in debates, and to play games that stimulated the mind. Marshall attended the Baltimore Colored High School. The school has been renamed Frederick Douglass High School.

He graduated from high school in 1925 and went to Lincoln University. His classmates at Lincoln included: Cab Calloway (jazz musician), Langston Hughes (author/poet), and Kwame Nkruma (the father of the African nation of Ghana).

187

GOD FIRST

Marshall graduated from Lincoln in 1930 and applied to the University of Maryland Law School. His application was denied, because they did not accept Black students. Marshall applied to Howard University in Washington, D.C. and was accepted.

Dean of Howard University's School of Law, Charles Houston, made sure that all of the school's law students became thoroughly acquainted with constitutional law. Marshall graduated from Howard in 1933 and started a law practice in Baltimore.

Soon after graduating from Howard, Marshall filed a petition against the segregation policies at the University of Maryland and won.

In 1934, Marshall became active in the NAACP and was their chief civil rights attorney from 1934 to 1961—challenging federal and state segregation laws dealing with housing, transportation, politics, criminal justice and education.

From 1940 to 1944 Marshall won 29 of 32 cases that he argued before the U.S. Supreme Court.

His hallmark victory came in 1954 when he convinced the U.S. Supreme Court that the educational policy of "Separate but Equal" was unconstitutional.

In 1961, President Kennedy appointed him as the first Black person to sit on the U.S. Court of Appeals. Because of his many victories in that position, he was appointed to the Second Court of Appeals that same year. In that position, he issued 112 rulings. ALL of which were upheld by the U.S. Supreme Court.

In 1965, President Johnson appointed him U.S. Solicitor General. Between 1965 and 1967, he won 14 of 19 civil rights cases for the government.

In 1967, President Johnson appointed him as the first Black judge to serve on the U.S. Supreme Court. Johnson said: "It's the *right time* to do the *right thing* with the *right man*."

WHAT DO THESE STONES MEAN?

Because of ill health, Marshall retired from the U.S. Supreme Court in 1991. Justice Marshall died in 1993, at the age of 84.

One of the greatest honors bestowed on him was being asked by the United Nations and the United Kingdom to draft the constitution for the emerging African nations of Ghana and Tanzania.

We thank God that Thurgood Marshall dedicated his life to *Seeking justice to Correcting oppression to Defending the fatherless and to Pleading for the widow.*

The protests of millions of people challenged the systems of segregation and discrimination, but it was the legal actions and decisions that made these practices illegal. Therefore, we're greatly indebted to the legal teams of the NAACP, the Congress of Racial Equality, and other groups. And we're especially grateful to people like Thurgood Marshall who took the fight from the streets to the courts—and won!

As Martin Luther King, Jr. once said:
"Laws can't make a man love me.
But they sure can make him think twice about lynching me."

Tombstones

Many of these acts of civil disobedience turned violent when white troopers hosed, beat, and ran down protesters with their horses. Many of these protesters were hospitalized and some of them were killed.

No one really knows how many people were killed during slavery and after slavery for protesting. There are monuments in at least two states to thousands of black men and women who were tortured and hanged by the Ku Klux Klan and other white supremacist individuals and groups.

In 1963, Medgar Evers (a man of peace who was president of the Mississippi state NAACP) was shot to death in his driveway. In 1963, four innocent black girls were killed by a bomb in their church. During the 1960s, many black and white men and women were killed while participating in non-violent protests. They included white people like

Rev. James Reeb and Viola Liuzzo. In April 1968 ("the apostle of non-violence"), Dr. Martin Luther King, Jr. was killed in Memphis, Tennessee.

CONCLUSION

People of all races, religions and cultures need to know about these stones. Black people in general—especially black children, black teenagers, and black young adults—need to know about these stones. People in general need to know about these stones.

Why?

Because these stones remind us that:
"Truth crushed to the ground will rise again."

These stones remind us that:
"We've come this far by faith. Leaning on the Lord. Trusting in His holy word."

These stones remind us that:
God has never failed us and that He never will!

QUESTIONS FOR REFLECTION & ACTION
After reading this sermon:

1. What did you learn from these stones of protest and these tombstones?
2. How did learning this (or being reminded of this) make you feel?
3. What events impressed you the most and why?
4. What individuals are you most grateful to and why?
5. What stones of protest still need to be laid and engaged in?

WHAT DO THESE STONES MEAN?
Joshua 4:1-7 (Part Three)

INTRODUCTION

In our last sermon, we looked at Stones of Protest and Tombstones. In this message, we will focus our attention on Stepping Stones.

In spite of the horrific conditions of slavery. In spite of the horrific conditions of segregation. In spite of racism and discrimination. In spite of being defined as 3/5 of a person. There have been some stepping stones.

Stepping stones are stones of progress. Let's look at some of these stepping stones of progress in the areas of sports, education, entertainment and politics.

Stepping Stones in the Area of Sports

Because of the laws of segregation, there was a time when Blacks were not allowed to participate against whites in any sport except boxing. Because Blacks were allowed to participate against whites in boxing, Jack Johnson became the first black heavyweight champion by defeating Jim Jeffries in 1901. After Johnson defeated Jeffries, every contender for the heavyweight crown was dubbed "The White Hope."

There was not another black heavyweight champion until Joe Louis knocked out James J. Braddock in 1937.

Louis reigned as heavyweight champion longer than anyone else. He was the undefeated heavyweight champion until he retired in 1949. During the years of his reign, there were several "White Hopes." The former heavyweight champion Max Baer attempted to take the crown from Louis but was knocked out. The light-heavyweight champion Billy Conn came close in their first fight but lost to Louis on a close decision. In their rematch, Louis knocked Conn out in the 8th. round. (I was at my radio listening to both fights).

GOD FIRST

Blacks were barred from other professional sports until Jackie Robinson broke the "color barrier" in baseball in 1947.

Because so many Blacks loved baseball and were good at it, there were special leagues formed in the 1800s and in the early 1900s for Blacks to play in. These teams were known as teams of the Negro League and produced some of the sport's greatest players.

According to many baseball experts, some of the greatest players to ever play the game were black players.

The Negro League didn't keep all of the statistics that the Major League kept, but they kept enough to let us know that the Negro League had some great players.

Satchel Paige was a premier pitcher. He was one of the best pitchers to ever play the game. He was almost 50 years old before he was allowed to play in the Major League. At that time, he was the oldest pitchers in the majors and one of the best. **Joe DiMaggio said that Paige was the best pitcher he ever faced. This was said about a man who was past his prime.**

Josh Gibson was definitely one of the greatest hitters of all time. In 1933, he played in 137 games. He hit 55 home runs and had a batting average of 467. In 1934, he hit 69 home runs.

Some sports commentators and experts called Gibson **"The Black Babe Ruth."** Other commentators and baseball experts called Ruth **"The White Josh Gibson."**

Gibson and Paige are just two of the many black players who have been inducted into the Negro League Hall of Fame.

Although Paige was past his prime, because he was able to pitch so effectively in the major league for several years, he was inducted into both the Negro League Hall of Fame and the Major League Hall of Fame. If more black players had been allowed to play in the major league, many more would have been in the major league hall of fame.

WHAT DO THESE STONES MEAN?

In all sports, not just in major league baseball, there have been some stepping stones for Blacks. Today, black players dominate professional basketball and professional football.

Stepping Stones in the Area of Education

One of the main things that whites did not want was for Blacks to be educated. Consequently, laws were passed in every state in the South prohibiting the education of Blacks.

In spite of these laws, a significant number of Blacks were able to be educated during slavery. The master of Phyllis Wheatley defied these laws and made sure that she got an education. As a result, Phyllis Wheatley not only became a great poet but also a great advocate for the abolition of slavery.

John Henry Meachum, a black pastor, created a Floating Freedom School on the Mississippi River in order to circumvent the anti-literacy laws against blacks in his state.

Through songs and stories by preachers and abolitionists and others, information and education was conveyed to many Blacks. Frederick Douglass said that the passage to freedom was to be able to read and write.

Booker T. Washington was blessed to be educated and dedicated himself to helping to educate as many Blacks as possible. His efforts resulted in establishing Tuskegee Institute in Tuskegee, Alabama.

In the late 1800s and early 1900s, after meeting with the black educator, Booker T. Washington, Julius Rosenwald created a fund to improve the education of black children in the South. By the time he died in 1932, Rosenwald had built more than 5300 schools for black children—primarily in rural areas of the South. These were known as "Rosenwald Schools."

Wilberforce University was the first Black school of higher education owned and operated by Black Americans. Howard University was the first Black law school. Spelman College was the first college for Black women.

Wiley College in Marshall, Texas, won many debate championships against black and white colleges that were larger and more prestigious. It's greatest achievement in this area was in defeating the reigning champion, University of Southern California, in 1935.

The movie, "The Great Debaters" was based upon this achievement. Although, in the movie, Harvard University (instead of the University of Southern California) was the school that they defeated and the place where the championship debate took place.

In 1962, James Meredith (under the protection of the National Guard) was the first black student to be admitted to the University of Mississippi.

In 1968, in spite of opposition from within and from without, San Francisco State University (from which I graduated in 1960 when it was known as San Francisco State College) was the first four-year college to establish a Black Studies Department. As a young pastor in the area, I supported those efforts publicly.

Stepping Stones in the Area of Entertainment

Singing and dancing are as natural to many black people as breathing (although I cannot sing a lick and I have two left feet).

Black Africans brought their music and their dancing with them when them came here as slaves. It was with this music, this singing, this dancing that they were free to amuse and entertain themselves and one another.

Slave owners and their families enjoyed this lively singing and dancing often came from "The Big House" to watch their slaves perform.

These slave owners and their families enjoyed watching these Black entertainers dance their dances and sing their songs.

During the period of Reconstruction these freed men and women pursued many avenues of vocation. Some of them became entertainers— first in their own circle of relatives and friends and black venues.

Black performers entertained in little clubs, in rural areas, in larger clubs in small cities, and eventually in large cities and venues like the great Apollo Theater in Harlem and in the clubs on the South side of Chicago and in many other major cities.

Many famous white entertainers came to these clubs and venues to watch, learn, take notes, be entertained, and imitate (as best they could) the unique styles of these transplanted Africans.

These Africanisms produced unique musical genres like jazz, the blues, rock-and-roll, the gospels, and the spirituals.

When white promoters learned of these great acts and saw these great entertainers, they began to sign them up to perform in their venues.

When these black entertainers were discovered, the world was able to see and hear such great musical entertainers as: Lena Horne, Marian Anderson, Count Basie, Cab Calloway, Nat King Cole, Billie Holliday, Ella Fitzgerald, Big Mama Thornton, Sammy Davis, Jr., Josephine Baker, Eartha Kitt, Smoky Robinson, Diana Ross, Tina Turner, Little Richard, Stevie Wonder, Johnnie Mathis, Lionel Hampton, Michael Jackson, Tupac, 50 Cent, James Brown, Chuck Berry, Fats Domino, B.B. King, Ray Charles, Jennifer Hudson, and Aretha Franklin.

The world has been able to see and be entertained by such black actors as: Hattie McDaniels, Sidney Poitier, Dorothy Dandridge, Dwayne "the Rock" Johnson, Samuel L. Jackson, Halle Berry, Oprah Winfrey, Ossie Davis, Ruby Dee, James Earl Jones, Olivia Spencer, Taraji J. Henson, Danny Glover, Snoop Dogg, Little Bow Wow, Viola Davis, Kerry Washington, and Denzel Washington.

Stepping Stones in the Area of Politics

Stepping stones in the area of politics started with the passages of the so-called Reconstruction Amendments to the Constitution. The 13th amendment that abolished slavery and made involuntary servitude illegal except in cases where one was being punished for a crime of which he had been convicted. The 14th and 15th amendments protected the rights of African Americans and gave Black men the right to vote and hold office.

After the Emancipation Proclamation and during the period of Reconstruction, many Blacks in the South were elected to city, state and national offices. Some were elected to congress. However, during the early 1900s, there were only a few black people elected to political offices. Today, there are thousands of black elected officials holding city, county, state, and national offices.

In 1966, Ed Brooke was elected a U.S. Senator from Massachusetts. In 1967, Carl Stokes was elected mayor of Cleveland and Richard Gordon Hatcher was elected mayor of Gary, Indiana.

In 1968, Shirley Chisholm became the first black woman to be elected to congress. In 1971, Thurgood Marshall became the first black person to serve as a justice of the U.S. Supreme Court. In 2008, Barack Obama was elected the 44th President of the United States.

These are just a few of the "Stepping Stones" for African Americans in the areas of sports and politics. We've come a long way. And we still have a long way to go.

CONCLUSION

In spite of racism. In spite of sexism. In spite of discrimination. In spite of slavery. In spite of segregation. In spite of "Jim Crow Laws." In spite of the Ku Klux Klan and the White Citizens Councils. In spite of "the skinheads" and alt-right. In spite of the John Birch Society and Citizens United. In spite of rapes, castrations, and hangings, there has been some progress.

There has been progress because the **GOD** of love, mercy, compassion, justice, and liberation has helped Blacks and whites, men and women to rise above circumstances and situations and **"make a way out of no way!"**

WHAT DO THESE STONES MEAN?

QUESTIONS FOR REFLECTION & ACTION
After reading this sermon:

1. What did you learn from this sermon?
2. What stepping stones do you feel were most important?
3. What stepping stones need to be added to this list?
4. What stepping stones do Black Americans need to make today?
5. What needs to be done to continue this process?
6. What are you willing to do to continue this process?

WHAT DO THESE STONES MEAN?
Joshua 4:1-7 (NIV) (Part Four)

INTRODUCTION

This is the final chapter of sermons on "What Do These Stones Mean?" We have looked at several significant stones related to the African American experience.

We have looked at **the Heritage Stone** that traced the origin of the human race and the history and culture of Black Americans back to "Mother Africa."

We have looked at **the Millstones of slavery and segregation** which robbed people of their freedom and attempted to destroy their dignity and self-worth.

We have looked at the **Stones of Protest** that were sometime verbal and sometime violent which helped to shed light on the desperate plight of Black Americans and help put an end to slavery and begin tearing down the walls of segregation and discrimination.

We have looked at some **Stepping Stones** in the areas of sports, education, entertainment, and politics that opened doors for black people with athletic abilities to participate in the sports they loved, for Blacks to be educated, for Blacks to become entertainers, and for Blacks to be elected to public offices where they could and would participate in making and enforcing the laws that govern our cities, states and nation.

In the final sermon in this series, we will look at a stone that is sometimes overlooked. It is not a stone in the sense of the other stones. This is a unique stone. It is the stone that gave people the courage and the insight and helped them to forge the other stones.

The Apostle Paul refers to this stone as "the chief cornerstone." The Apostle James refers to this stone as "the living stone."

WHAT DO THESE STONES MEAN?

The Living Stone

In Ephesians 2:19-20, the Apostle Paul refers to believers as *"fellow citizens with God's people and members of God's household, built on the foundation of the apostles and prophets, with Christ Jesus himself as the chief cornerstone." (NIV)*

In 1 Peter 2:4, the Apostle Peter refers to Christ as *"the living stone— rejected by men but chosen by God and precious to him." (NIV)*

The stone that the builders rejected is the chief cornerstone. The chief cornerstone is the living stone. This stone is not an object. This stone is a person.

This stone has been referred to as "a rock in a weary land." This stone has been referred to as "a shelter in the time of storm."

According to the Scriptures, this Living Stone had no beginning and will have no ending. John tells us this in the prologue to his gospel:

In the beginning was the Word, and the Word was with God, and the Word was God. He was in the beginning with God. Through him all things were made that have been made. In him was life, and that life was the light of men. And the light shines in the darkness, but the darkness has not understood it (KJV – could not put it out). (John 1:1-5)

In verses 10-14, John continues by telling us that:

He was in the world, and though the world was made through him, the world did not recognize him. He came to that which was his own, but his own did not receive him. Yet to all who received him, to those who believed in his name, he gave the right to become children of God --- children born not of natural descent, nor of human wisdom nor of a husband's will, but born of God.

The Word became flesh and made his dwelling among us. We beheld his glory, the glory of the One and Only, who came from the Father, full of grace and truth. (NIV)

According to Luke 4:14-19:

Jesus returned to Galilee in the power of the Spirit, and news about him spread through the whole countryside. He taught in their synagogue, and everyone praised him. He went to Nazareth, where he had been brought up, and on the Sabbath day he went into the synagogue, as was his custom. And he stood up to read. The scroll of the prophet Isaiah was handed to him. Unrolling it, he found the place where it is written: 'The Spirit of the Lord is on me, because he has anointed me to preach good news to the poor. He sent me to proclaim freedom to the prisoners, and recovery of sight for the blind, to release the oppressed, to proclaim the year of the Lord's favor. (NIV)

The King James Version of these verses says that Jesus came to *"set at liberty those who are oppressed"* and to *"set the captives free."*

Both versions make it clear that Jesus is declaring that He came to set people free. From these and other verses of Scripture it is clear that Jesus came to set people free physically, mentally, and spiritually.

Jesus came to set people free totally. Jesus came to set people free from anything and from everything ungodly, such as the influence and power of Satan. Jesus came to set people free from everything that keeps them from knowing and doing God's will, from everything that keeps them from loving God with all their heart, and from loving their neighbor as they do themselves.

People who are enslaved are captives physically and emotionally. People who do the enslaving can do so because they are either enslaved spiritually or because they have at least a temporary spiritual "blind spot." That's why the writer of Amazing Grace said: "I was blind. But now I see."

WHAT DO THESE STONES MEAN?

Because Jesus came to "set at liberty those who are oppressed" and to "set the captives free," Jesus was working **on, in, and through people** who were involved in ending slavery and segregation and in promoting justice and equality.

Jesus Christ, the Son of the Living God, is the Living Stone.

This Living Stone is both human and divine. This Living Stone is both fully human and fully divine.

In His humanity, this Stone was born in Bethlehem. This Stone was baptized in the Jordan River. This Stone stopped by a marriage feast in Cana and turned water into wine. This Stone walked on the Sea of Galilee. This Stone went about doing good—healing the sick, giving sight to the blind, unstopping deaf ears, causing the lame to walk, the dumb to talk. This Stone took two small fish and five loaves of bread and fed 5,000 men plus women and children and had twelve baskets of fragments left over. This Stone raised the dead.

This Stone is the Son of God and the Savior of the world. This Stone is the Wonderful Counselor, the Mighty God, the Everlasting Father, and the Prince of Peace.

This Stone is the Good Shepherd, the Door to the Sheep, and the Lamb of God who came to take away the sins of the world. This Stone is the Way, the Truth, and the Life. This Stone is the Resurrection and the Life.

This Stone went to the Cross and suffered, bled, and died on the Cross for you and me. This Stone died on the Cross for the sins of the world.

This Stone stayed in the grave all night Friday night. This Stone stayed in the grave all day Saturday. This Stone stayed in the grave all night Saturday night.

But early Sunday morning, this Stone got up from the grave. This Stone pulled the sting out of death. This Stone robbed the grave of its victory. This Stone declared for all eternity, "All power of heaven and earth is in my hands!"

This Stone is the Capstone and the Main Stone. This Stone is the stone that made the work and the results of the other stones possible.

This Stone made the Heritage Stone possible. This Stone made breaking the chains of the Millstones possible. This Stone made the courage and the results of the Protest Stones and the Tombstones possible. This Stone made the Stepping Stones possible. This Stone is the Living Stone—the Stone that the builders rejected. This Stone is Jesus Christ. This Stone is the Son of the Living God. This Stone is the Savior of the world.

"What Do These Stones Mean?"

These stones mean that:
"The Lord is good. His mercy is everlasting.
And His truth endures to all generations!"
(Psalm 100:5, KJV)

QUESTIONS FOR REFLECTION & ACTION
After reading this sermon:

1. What influence did the Living Stone have on these other stones?
2. Why do you think this was so?
3. What influence does the Living Stone have in your life?
4. What influence would you like for the Living Stone to have in your life?
5. What influence would you like for the Living Stone to have in your relatives and friends?
6. What influence would you like for the Living Stone to have in people throughout the country and around the world?
7. What are you willing to do to help make this happen?
8. When will you start?

CHAPTER SIX

GOING TO THE NEXT LEVEL

"Responses to Racism"
"Repentance That Leads to Social Justice & Racial Reconciliation"
"What Racial Reconciliation Looks Like"
"God First for a Better Life"

RESPONSES TO RACISM

John 4:1-26 (NIV)

As we begin this final chapter of sermons, we will be focusing our attention on Going to the Next Level in our spiritual growth and development. As we begin this journey, let's take a look at racism and responses to racism. As we do so, let's begin by defining racism.

What is Racism?

Some people may tell you that they may not be able to define racism, but they certainly recognize it when they see it.

As I reflect on racism, three basic observations come to mind. Based on these reflections, I would like to define racism in three basic statements:

(1) Any attitude or practice of racial discrimination

(2) Any practice that seek to keep races separated from each other

(3) The belief that one race is superior to another

GOD FIRST

Jesus Responds to Racism

In our text, Jesus responds to the woman of Samaria who refused to draw some water from Jacob's well and give Him a drink because He was a Jew. For many years, Jews and Samaritans had animosity toward each other.

This animosity was **racial** because Samaritans were a mixed breed of Jew and Gentile who had intermarried, and the Jews felt that these half-breeds were inferior to them. This animosity was **religious** because some of these Samaritans had previously worshiped idol gods and were still doing so, although they believe in parts of the Hebrew bible and also worshiped Yahweh.

In order to avoid having any unnecessary contact with one another, Jews lived in the north and south and the Samaritans lived in the central region of Palestine. Both groups practiced racial discrimination and the Jews had a superiority complex.

Because Jesus wanted the Samaritans to know that He was the promised Messiah **and** because He wanted to break down the wall of animosity between Jews and Samaritans, He felt compelled to go through Samaria in order to encounter the woman in our text, engage her in conversation, and reveal Himself to her as the Messiah so that she would go to the town of Sychar and tell the people that she had met the Promised Messiah.

As a result of this woman's testimony, many Samaritans believed in Jesus. When these Samaritans went to meet Jesus and invited Him to stay with them for two days, many more Samaritans became believers and were able to say: *"now we have heard for ourselves, and we know that this man really is the Savior of the world."* (John 4:42)

My Grandfather's Response to An Insult to My Mother

As I look back over personal experiences, I thank God for being raised in a family that was built on a foundation of biblical principles.

My maternal grandfather, Sip Jeremiah Colvin, required everyone to repeat Proverbs 3:5-6 at each meal:

"Trust in the Lord with all thine heart.
Lean not to thine own understanding.
In all thy ways acknowledge Him.
He shall direct thy paths."
(Proverbs 3:5-6, KJV)

Although Papa had only about a fifth-grade education, he was blessed to have his own roofing business that employed about a dozen men.

Papa was also a man of great spiritual and moral integrity who would take a stand against anyone (black or white) on issues of injustice and inequality.

My mother served as an Army nurse during the Second World War and earned the rank of Second Lieutenant. When I was about 8 years old, mother came home to Terrell, Texas, on furlough and was insulted by an employee at the train station. She came home and told the family about the incident. The whole family was upset—especially my grandfather.

After hearing her story, Papa took mother by the hand and went to his car—a black Dodge—and headed to the train station. The word spread quickly that Papa was "going to the train station to see the white man who insulted Hattie Ellen."

Family members got into cars and headed to the train station. When we got there, Papa and mother had gone inside and we decided to park outside and wait in the cars.

After about an hour or so, Papa and mother came out and got into his Dodge and drove home. No one said a word. I never heard what happened inside the train station. But I believe that my grandfather didn't leave until he got the apology that he wanted for my mother. All of us were proud that Papa took a stand for his daughter.

My Response to a Racist Statement in Hammond, Indiana

Some of that "spunk" probably rubbed off on me. During the 1960s, I attended civil rights rallies and participated in civil rights demonstrations for fair housing and employment in San Francisco. Martin Luther King, Jr. and Ralph David Abernathy were a part of some of those rallies.

In 1970, Hammond, Indiana, was a city of 100,000 with a 96% white population and a 4% black population that, except for one black family, was limited to living in the part of the city known as East Hammond.

When I became Executive Director of Brooks House of Christian Service in Hammond, we were able to purchase a house a few blocks north of East Hammond that was owned by the Indiana Baptist Convention and lived in by my white predecessor.

Fortunately, we had good relationships with our white neighbors. I had many friendly conversations with my white neighbor who lived across the street and was a member of the 15,000-member First Baptist Church that owned over two hundred buses that picked up people (mainly children, even a few from East Hammond) for Sunday School.

One day, in my conversation with my neighbor across the street, I mentioned that my family and I would like to worship at his church one Sunday.

This caught him by surprise. After he collected himself, he said to me: **"Colvin, you and your family would be more comfortable at Mt. Zion."**

Then I replied: **"No, YOU would be more comfortable if my family worshiped at Mt. Zion."**

Mt. Zion was a black congregation in East Hammond

My Response to a Racial Slur in Gary, Indiana

In one of my previous sermons, I mentioned the situation when a white service station worker (the brother of the owner) called one of my members a "nigger." When I went over to confront him about this and asked him to apologize to my member, he refused to do so because he said he had heard black people using this word to each other.

Because he refused to apologize, I called and sent a letter to Shell's corporate office and sent a letter to local media. The two black weekly newspapers published my letter on their front page.

The next Saturday, dozens of members of our church boycotted the station. Within a few weeks, the station was closed.

My Response to a Racist Statement by Black Politicians in Gary, Indiana

In one of my pervious sermons, I also noted that when a white city councilman decided to run for mayor in a city that was more than 90% black and had had two black mayors who had served a total of seven terms, some black politicians urged black people not to vote for him because he was white.

When I read their statements, I publicly denounced their statements as racist. I reminded people of the statement of Dr. King that:

a person should not be judged by the color of his skin but by the content of his character

Although I received flak from a few politicians, the white candidate won overwhelmingly and was re-elected.

General Observation

Segregation in general and redlining in particular have been (and still are) efforts to keep races apart in our society.

The other form of racism mentioned in my definition is the belief that one race is superior to another. This was a basic belief of the Nazi party in Germany and of white supremacist groups like the Ku Klux Klan, the Skinheads, the Alt-right, the Neo-Nazis, white citizen's councils, and other white supremacist groups in the United States.

The Response of Daryl Davis to the Klan

My wife likes to watch talk shows. One day she was watching THE TALK when the discussion was about a man by the name of Daryl Davis. As she listened to the discussion, she became interested in learning more about him. She googled his name and learned that for thirty years, a black blues musician has spent time befriending members of the Ku Klux Klan. In an interview, Daryl describes his first meeting with a Klansman.

According to the interview, Daryl was playing in a club when a white fellow came up and told him that he had never heard a black man play a piano like Jerry Lee Lewis. Daryl told the man that Jerry Lee Lewis learned to play like that from listening to black blues and boogie-woogie musicians like Fats Domino and Little Richard. The man was shocked to hear this and decided to sit down and have a drink with Daryl.

During the conversation, the man told Daryl that he was a member of the Ku Klux Klan and that he had never sat down and had a drink with a black man before because he and the Klan knew that black people were inferior and that they had a gene that made them serial killers.

Daryl was shocked to hear this and told the man that he wasn't a serial killer. The man responded by telling Daryl that his gene was just latent and hadn't come out yet. Daryl asked the man to name one black serial killer. He could not think of one.

Daryl searched for a good comeback and finally told the man that white people were the ones who had a gene that makes them serial killers. He went on to name several white serial killers. The man said that he didn't have that gene because he had never killed anyone. Daryl told the man that's because his gene is latent. It just hadn't come out yet.

Obviously, the man got the point because five months later he gave Daryl his Klan robe and told him that he had given up his membership in the Klan.

Daryl decided to go around the country and sit down with as many Klan leaders as possible, have a drink with them and a friendly conversation

GOING TO THE NEXT LEVEL

in order to get to know them. According to the interview, as of that date, **three hundred Klansmen** had given him their robe.

CONCLUSION

Racism is a poison and needs to be eradicated. Laws cannot end racism because racism is in the heart. Only the grace of God, through His Holy Spirit, can help people to get rid of their racism.

My prayer is that every man and woman and every boy and girl in our society and around the world will ask the Lord to **search them** and **help them** MOVE RACISM out of their minds and heart. Anyone can do this. As the hymn says:

> **"ASK the Savior to help you.**
> **COMFORT, strengthen and keep you.**
> **HE is willing to aid you.**
> **HE will carry you through."**[12]

QUESTIONS FOR REFLECTION & ACTION
After reading this sermon:

1. What did you learn from this message?
2. How did learning this make you feel?
3. What do you think of these examples of racism?
4. What do you think especially of the experience of Daryl Davis and the Klan?
5. What has been some of your experiences with racism?
6. How did you respond?
7. How would you hope that everyone would respond to racism?
8. What are some things that can and should be done to eliminate racism?
9. Which of these things are you willing to do and when will you start doing them?

---

12 The New National Baptist Hymnal.

REPENTANCE THAT LEADS TO SOCIAL JUSTICE & RACIAL RECONCILIATION

Isaiah 1:10-17 (NIV)

As we turn our attention to the second sermon in this chapter, let's look at the need for repentance that leads to social justice and racial reconciliation. We do so because racial reconciliation must begin with repentance and repentance must lead to social justice. Therefore, let's begin by looking at repentance.

In Isaiah 1:10-17, the prophet of God condemns the people of Judah for their shallow religious observances and challenges them to seek justice, to correct oppression, to defend the fatherless, and to plead for the widow. The prophet suggests that doing this would be an act of repentance that would lead to social justice. I contend that repentance that leads to social justice will also lead to racial reconciliation.

REPENTANCE

The word repent or repentance is used more than a hundred times in the Bible. Some of the key verses on repentance are: Jeremiah 15:19, Matthew 3:8, Matthew 4:17, Luke 3:1-14, Luke 5:27-32, Luke 13:1-9, Luke 17:1-4, and Acts 17:30.

One of the best statements on repentance that I have found is in R.C. Sproul's little booklet, "What Is Repentance?" In this little 37-page booklet, Sproul examines the basic Greek and Hebrew words for repentance and looks at Old Testament and New Testament Scriptures on repentance. In the Old Testament, Sproul notes that:

> "True repentance was to be expressed with the lament, a song of grief, and accompanied by loud cries and wailing… In addition, specific prayers were part of the religious system of Israel…The most famous of the penitent psalms is Psalm 51…A final feature of this ritualistic life were special days

GOING TO THE NEXT LEVEL

of repentance. These days were set apart not only for feasts, celebrations and remembrances of the past, but also for penitence."[13]

In his focus on Psalm 51, Sproul makes the following observation.

"It's important to see the anguish and heartfelt remorse expressed by David, but we must also understand that repentance of the heart is the work of God the Holy Spirit... The Holy Spirit demonstrates in Psalm 51 how He produces repentance in our hearts."[14]

Consequently, it is the Holy Spirit who produces repentance in us and through us. This is clear from verses 9 and 10 where David says: "Create in me a clean heart, O God, and renew a right spirit within me."

Sproul notes that "The only way to have a clean heart is by a work of divine re-creation."[15]

David makes this even clearer in verse 11 where he says, "Cast me not away from thy presence, and take not your holy spirit from me." (KJV)

Based upon these and other Scriptures, to repent is to have a change of attitude, a change of heart, and a change of mind that causes one to go in a new direction as a result of the leading, guiding, directing, and empowering of the Holy Spirit.

Based upon these and other Scriptures, to repent is to realize that one has committed a sin against God or against another person. Once they are convicted of that sin by the Holy Spirit, the goal is to make a conscious decision, with the help of the Holy Spirit to not repeat it. Therefore, repentance begins with acknowledgement that moves one to

---

13 R. C. SPROUL, What Is Repentance? (Ligonier Ministries, 2019), 6-7.

14 Ibid., 21.

15 Ibid., 25.

take action under the leading, guiding, directing, and empowering of the Holy Spirit.

A classic example of repentance is found in Luke 19:1-10 where Zacchaeus the tax collector repented of his sin against those he had cheated and was willing to make restitution.

The key to this classic example is that repentance is more than just an attitude or a feeling. Repentance is an **action** that one takes as a result of being convicted of his or her sin against God or against another person.

In her book, *Real: The Surprising Secret to Deeper Relationships*, Catherine Parks lists eight steps that she believes are suggested in Psalm 51 for real repentance. (1) Define the sin (2) Appeal to God's mercy (3) Avoid defensiveness and see God rightly (4) Look to Jesus (5) Ask God to break you and heal you (6) Be comforted by the Spirit (7) Rejoice and proclaim truth (8) Resolve to obey.[16]

SOCIAL JUSTICE
Biblical Foundation

The theme of social justice is echoed throughout the Bible. This theme is found in many passages in both the Old and the New Testament.

In the Old Testament, the Lord God sent Moses to Egypt to be the deliverer of the Jewish people who had been enslaved for more than four hundred years. When Moses went to Egypt, he told Pharaoh, the ruler of Egypt, that the Lord God of the universe said, "Let my people go."

In Isaiah 1:17, the Lord God told His people through the prophet Isaiah to "Seek justice. Correct oppression. Defend the fatherless. Plead for the widow."

In Amos 5: 21-24, the Lord God told His people through His prophet that He rejected their empty worship because of their lack of compassion and social justice.

---

16   Catherine Parks, Real; The Surprising Secret To Deeper Relationships (The Good Book Company, 2018).

I hate, I despise your religious feasts; I cannot stand your assemblies. Even though you bring me burnt offerings and grain offerings, I will not accept them. Though you bring choice fellowship offerings, I will have no regard for them. Away with the noise of your songs! I will not listen to the music of your harps. But let justice roll on like a river and righteousness like a never-failing stream. (Amos 5:21-24, NIV)

According to Luke 4:18-19, when our Lord Jesus Christ returned to Nazareth he went into the synagogue and proclaimed from the scroll of the prophet Isaiah:

"The Spirit of the Lord is on me, because he has anointed me to preach Good news to the poor. He has sent me to proclaim freedom for the prisoners and recovery of sight for the blind, to release the oppressed, to proclaim the year of the Lord's favor." (NIV)

These and other passages of Scripture remind us that our God is a God of justice and liberation. He is a God of freedom and liberty. He is a God of mercy and compassion. And He expects His people to emulate Him.

Biblical Examples of Social Justice

Many men and women of faith have engaged in efforts to acquire social justice for people who were being denied it. Moses, Isaiah, and Amos were champions for social justice. Moses was God's deliverer of the children of Israel from bondage in Egypt. Isaiah and Amos issued strong pronouncements to the children of Israel regarding their responsibility to be engage in acts of social justice. Jesus, the One anointed by God to be the Savior of the world, at the beginning of His ministry affirmed that He had come to fulfill the prophetic pronouncement of Isaiah to set the captives free.

Historical Actions for Social Justice

As we view the pages of history, we see many men and women (some of our faith and some of other faiths) who have engaged in efforts for social justice.

Because the revolutionary war was about personal, social, and political freedom those who fought in it (Blacks and Whites) and those who supported it in other ways (Blacks and Whites, men and women) were doing so in order to acquire social justice.

Because the civil war was about personal, social and political freedom those who fought in it (Blacks and Whites) and those who supported it in other ways (Blacks and Whites, men and women) were doing so in order to achieve social justice.

Over in England, William Wilberforce was joined by his pastor, John Newton (a former slave trader who, after being convicted of the sin of slavery, wrote "Amazing Grace") by Olaudah Equiano (a former slave who became a best-selling author and bought his freedom) and by many others during his twenty-year quest to end the slave trade in the British empire.

Lerone Bennett, in his classic book, *Pioneers in Protest*, lists many black and white people who have been champions for social justice and racial equality. Bennett describes William Lloyd Garrison as "The apostle of nonviolence … a fiery white editor who shared leadership of the militant abolitionist wing with several Blacks and with radicals, including Wendell Phillips, the Boston blueblood who gave up his place and position and dedicated himself heart and soul to the struggle for black rights."[17]

The list of champions for freedom and equality as a part of a total package of social justice must include people such as Frederick Douglass, W.E.B. DuBois, Sojourner Truth, Harriet Tubman, Mary White Ovington, Booker T. Washington, Charles Sumner, and Thaddeus Stevens, as well as people like John Brown and Nat Turner.

---

17   Lerone Bennett, Pioneers in Protest (Baltimore: Penguin Books Inc, 1969), 101.

Contemporary Actions for Social Justice

When we consider contemporary contributions to the cause of social justice, we must begin with the National Association for the Advancement of Colored People (the N.A.A.C.P), which was founded in 1909 and is the oldest, and possibly the largest, civil rights group in America. It's most ardent champion for most of those years was Thurgood Marshall, who argued landmark cases before the Supreme Court and won almost all of them.

We must also consider the work of other civil rights groups like the Congress of Racial Equality (C.O.R.E.), the Student Nonviolent Coordinating Committee (SNCC), People United to Save Humanity (PUSH), and Common Cause. We also need to consider criminal justice reform groups like Southern Poverty Law Center (SPLC) and restorative justice groups. We're indebted to religious groups like the Southern Christian Leadership Council (SCLC), the African American Christian Clergy Coalition (AACCC), the Arizona Faith Network, Evangelicals for Social Action, Sojourners. the New Poor People's Campaign, and KAIROS The Center for Religions, Rights, and Social Justice.

Prominent individuals who have been champions for social justice include Martin Luther King, Jr., Fannie Lou Hamer, Rosa Park, Diane Nash, John Lewis, Jessie Jackson, Al Sharpton, William Barber, Nelson Mandela, and Barack Obama (who was a community organizer for social justice and racial equality long before he entered the political arena).

When Barack Obama was working with the Gamaliel Foundation in Illinois back in the late eighties and early nineties, one Saturday morning he gave a dynamic presentation at a church in East Chicago, Indiana for a community organization called L.I.F.T. (Lake Interfaith Families Together) of which I was a founding member. The organization was comprised of some 40 Protestant and Catholic churches throughout Lake County Indiana that was formed to address social issues in our communities and throughout the county. Several members of our church

GOD FIRST

were at the meeting along with people from other churches. At the end of his presentation people were heard saying: "That young man is going places!" And, indeed he did!

CONCLUSION

In his book, *Let's Get to Know Each Other*, Dr. Tony Evans reminds us that the church also has a social responsibility to the broader non-Christian society.

> "Therefore, as we have opportunity, let us do good to all, especially to those who are of the household of faith." (Gal. 6:10). While this is secondary, it is nevertheless, the responsibility of the church to 'speak the truth' about the sin of oppression to the whole culture.[18]

In light of the apostles' statement in Acts 5:29, "We ought to obey God rather than men," Evans contends that:

> "This shows us that whenever a religious or civil ruling body... contradicts what God has said or commanded, we are to disobey its laws.... In addition, when the Government fails to fulfill its divine responsibility of promoting justice (Rom. 13:1-5), then Christians have the right and responsibility to resist, as long as such resistance is within Christian behavior."[19]

Understanding this has been at the heart of movements throughout history to work for justice and equality. As we face the social challenges of our day, we need to engage in peaceful and productive social actions that help us to create a society where there is indeed liberty and justice for all!

---

18 Tony Evans, Let's Get to Know Each Other (Nashville: T. Nelson, 1995), 77.

19 Ibid., 77-78,

GOING TO THE NEXT LEVEL

QUESTIONS FOR REFLECTION & ACTION
After reading this sermon:

1. What did you learn from this message?
2. How did learning this make you feel?
3. What are some things we can do as acts of repentance?
4. What are some of the social issues that need to be addressed?
5. Why and how do you feel they need to be addressed?
6. Which issue or issues are you willing to address?
7. When will you start?
8. What issues are you willing to encourage others to address?

WHAT RACIAL RECONCILIATION LOOKS LIKE

Ephesians 2:13-22 (NIV)

The Apostle Paul begins Ephesians chapter two by reminding Jewish believers that they were once dead in their sins but have been made alive in Christ. In verses 13 through 22, he reminds Gentile believers that:

> *But now in Christ Jesus you who once were far away have been brought near Through the blood of Christ. For he himself is our peace, who has made the two one and has destroyed the barrier, the dividing wall of hostility, by abolishing in his flesh the law with its commandments and regulations. His purpose was to create in himself one new man out of the two, thus making peace, and in this one body to reconcile both of them to God through the cross, by which he put to death their hostility. He came and preached peace to those of you who were far away peace to those who were near. For through him we both have access to the Father by one Spirit. Consequently, you are no longer foreigners and aliens, but fellow citizens with God's people and members of God's household, built on the foundation of the apostles and the prophets, with Jesus Christ himself as the chief cornerstone. In him the whole building is joined together and rises to become a holy temple in the Lord. And in him you too are being built together to become a holy temple in the Lord. And in him you too are being built together to become a dwelling in which God lives by his spirit. (NIV)*

These verses make it abundantly clear that racial reconciliation between Jews and Gentiles was of paramount importance to our Lord Jesus Christ.

In light of these verses, I believe that racial reconciliation between Blacks and Whites and between other groups is of paramount importance to the Lord today.

However, before there can be racial reconciliation there must be repentance that leads to social justice.

White Americans must acknowledge and take responsibility for creating and perpetuating a system of racial animosity, mistrust, injustice and inequality that is rooted and grounded in the ignorance that has perpetuated the concept of white superiority and black inferiority.

Black Americans must be willing to enter into dialogue with and work with White Americans to create a better future for all Americans. This will not be easy for some Black Americans because of the mistrust they have for white people. Hopefully, most Black Americans, especially those of the Christian community, will step out in faith to help tear down the walls of division and help build the necessary avenues of cooperation.

As both Blacks and Whites see progress being made more of them will be willing to join these efforts in order to help move toward the goal of "liberty and justice for all."

In his book, *Let's Get to Know Each Other,*" Tony Evans says:

Somehow, the conservative white Christian did not actualize the truth of Ephesians 2:14: 'For He Himself is our peace, who has made both one, and thus broken down the middle wall of separation.' White evangelical theologians understood well the theology of Ephesians 4, but functioned as though these instructions had been given by Immanuel Kant and not the apostle Paul through the agency of the Holy Spirit.

Unfortunately, some black evangelicals made the mistake of viewing their own history, culture, and the church through the lens of the white theology. This was a disaster, as many joined whites in assessing black Christians as being 'that ignorant, uneducated, overemotional group of people.' These Blacks alienated themselves from the very community that gave them birth and the one that needed their own expertise. And they themselves were caught in a matrix of confusion because they had been taught to be biblical before being cultural.[20]

As I reflect upon the issue of racial reconciliation, I'm convinced that when it comes to race relations in general and to the need for racial reconciliation, some people just "don't get it." Some people wonder and don't understand "what the fuss is all about?"

Some people "get it," but they don't know what to do or where to start. Because the challenge to recognize the need for racial reconciliation and to do something about racial conciliation is so great and so important, I have spent much time thinking about it and praying about it. After much prayerful deliberation, I am convinced that most people won't understand what to do until they **understand** and **internalize** the implication of two biblical principles: "The Golden Rule" and "The Jesus Rule."

"The Golden Rule"
Matthew 7:12

Most people, believers and non-believers, know the golden rule. They can recite it verbatim: "Do unto others as you want them to do unto you."

This paraphrase of what we call "the Golden Rule" is based on the statement of Jesus found in Matthew 7:12.

In Matthew 7:12, Jesus says: *"So in everything, do to others what you would have them do to you, for this sums up the Law and the Prophets."*

Note the first three word:
"So in everything."

Everything means EVERYTHING! Everything means "everything you THINK." Everything means "Everything you SAY." Everything means 'Everything you DO."

---

20   Ibid., 108.

GOING TO THE NEXT LEVEL

In order to understand this statement from Jesus, you need to **personalize** it. In order to understand this statement from Jesus, you need to **internalize** it.

When you **personalize** and **internalize** this statement from Jesus, before you think anything about another person, ask yourself,

"Do I want anyone to **think** this way about **ME**?"
"Do I want anyone to **think** about **ME** in this way?"

When you **personalize** and **internalize** this statement from Jesus, before you **say** anything to or about another person, ask yourself, "would I want anyone to **say** this to **ME**?" "Do I want anyone to **say** this to or say this about **ME**?

When you **personalize** and **internalize** this statement from Jesus, before you **do** anything to someone else, ask yourself, "Would I want anyone to **do** this to **ME**?

If the answer is NO,
YOU should ask the Lord to help you to NOT think this of anyone else or think of anyone else in this way

If the answer is NO,
YOU should ask the Lord to help you to NOT say this to or about anyone else

If the answer is NO,
YOU should ask the Lord to help you to NOT do this to anyone else

As you think about these and other questions, put yourself in the other person's place and ask yourself would you want anyone to **think** about you in this way? Would you want anyone to **say** this to or about you? Would you want anyone to **do** this to you?

If you're serious about fostering racial reconciliation, **personalize** and **internalize** this statement from Jesus. If you're serious about fostering racial reconciliation, personalize and internalize "the Golden rule."

"The Jesus Rule"
Matthew 25:40 & Matthew 25:45

In order to foster racial reconciliation, the other biblical principle that needs to be personalized and internalized also comes from Jesus. I call this principle "The Jesus Rule" and it is expressed in Matthew 25:40 and in Matthew 25:45.

In Matthew 25:40 Jesus says:
**"Whatever you did for one of the least
of these brothers of mine,
you did for Me."**

In this parable, Jesus describes Himself as the Son of Man and the King of Glory who will judge the nations of the world by how they treated people in need of food, clothing, and shelter, as well as on how they treated those who were sick and in prison.

According to verses 32, the righteous Judge will "separate the people from one another as a shepherd separates the sheep from the goats." According to verses 33-40, the righteous sheep will be placed on His right hand and will receive their blessed inheritance because of how they responded to the needs, the condition, and the plight of others.

In verse 40, Jesus says whatever you did **to** and **for** the least of these you did to and for Me. This suggests that Jesus takes **personally** the things that we do to and for others.

GOING TO THE NEXT LEVEL

In verses 41 to 46 the righteous Judge turns to the goats on His left. He tells these people to "depart from me" because of how you did not respond to the needs, the condition, and the plight of others.

In verse 45 Jesus tells them:

"whatever you did not do for one of the least of these, you did not do for Me." (NIV)

Again, Jesus takes this **personally**. Jesus takes **personally** what we don't do for others. If Jesus takes it **personally** when we **fail** to **respond** to the needs, the condition, and the plight of others, then a lot individuals, a lot of churches, a lot of denominations, a lot of governments, a lot of other institutions, and a lot of nations have a lot to answer for.

God's Word says: "**Seek justice. Correct oppression. Defend the fatherless. Plead for the widow**" (Isaiah 1:17 KJV).

When we fail to seek justice,
Jesus says "You failed to do that for Me."

When we fail to correct oppression,
Jesus says: "You failed to do that for Me."

When we fail to defend the fatherless,
Jesus says: "You failed to do that for Me."

When we fail to plead for the widow,
Jesus says, "You failed to do that for Me."

This realization should cause believers to repent and to start doing things to help eliminate racism, sexism, unjust laws, unfair punishment, double standards, and all other expressions of political, economic, educational, judicial, structural, and institutional oppression, repression, and suppression. The results will create a society where there is truly "liberty and justice for all."

Several recent books that have become movies have highlighted some significant things that have happened as a result of repentance that led to social justice and racial reconciliation.

Just Mercy, by Brian Stevenson depicts the efforts of Brian Stevenson, a Harvard Law School graduate, who traveled to Alabama in 1989 to found the Equal Justice Initiative to help fight for poor people (black and white) who cannot afford legal representation. Stevenson teams up with a young white activist, Eva Ansley, and travels to an Alabama prison to meet its death row inmates. He meets Walter "Johnny D." McMillian, an African-American man who was convicted of the 1986 murder of a white woman named Ronda Morrison. After studying his case, Stevenson realizes that McMillian's conviction hinged on the testimony of a white convicted felon, Ralph Myers, who provided highly self-contradictory testimony in exchange for a lighter sentence.

Myers, who was on death row, admitted that he was coerced by local police who played on his fear of being burned by threatening to have him executed in the electric chair.

Stevenson was able to convince Myers to recant his testimony and appealed to the local court to give McMillian a new trial. Thirty days after Myers recanted his testimony, the judge ruled that Myers' initial testimony would stand because he had been coerced by the defense to recant his testimony.

In his frustration, Stevenson appears on *60 Minutes* in an effort to rally public support to get a new trial for McMillian before the Alabama Supreme Court. The court overturns McMillian's previous conviction and grants a new trial.

Before the trial, Stevenson meets with prosecutor, Tommy Chapman, in an effort to convince him to review his notes and join him in a motion

GOING TO THE NEXT LEVEL

to drop the charges against McMillian. Chapman refuses to even look at Stevenson's notes.

On the day of the new trial, after Stevenson presents compelling evidence as to why the charges against McMillian should be dropped, Chapman agrees to join him in his motion. The case is dismissed. After being in prison for several years for a crime he didn't commit (and a significant amount of that time on death row), McMillian was united with his family.[21]

This is a great example of repentance that leads to social justice.

The Best of *Enemies: Race and Redemption in the New South* by Osha Gray Davidson is a moving account of the unexpected friendship that emerged between Black activist Ann Atwater and C.P. Ellis, the white Exalted Cyclops of the North Carolina Branch of the Ku Klux Klan.

Ann Atwater, a Black domestic, became a community organizer and spokesperson for the Black community. C. P. Ellis, a poor White laborer was a prominent spokesman for poor whites and believed strongly in racial segregation.

The issue is school segregation. Blacks want to integrate their school with the White school while the Whites want the Blacks to "stay in their place" and stay in their own school.

The problem becomes more intense when the Black school is severely damaged by fire. Classes had to be staggered and many other adjustments had to be made because of the condition of the building.

In order to get input from the Black and the White communities, a city official decided to secure the services of someone from the outside to come to Durham and conduct a charrette—a series of meetings where

---

21 Bryan Stevenson, Just Mercy: a Story of Justice and Redemption (Melbourne: Scribe, 2020).

GOD FIRST

Blacks and Whites met separately for several days to discuss perceived pros and cons regarding school segregation and integration; then come together to report their findings and vote on each proposal coming from each racial group.

At the end of the charrette, a slim majority of the participants voted for school integration. This was a great surprise to many, because C.P. Ellis was able to cast a deciding vote.

During the days of meeting separately and meeting together, Ellis learned, to his surprise, that he and many black parents shared many of the same fears and concerns.

This led to an eventual estrangement between Ellis and the Klan and led to a growing friendship with Atwater.

A key factor in fostering this new relationship was that Atwater went to see Ellis' mentally challenged son in the hospital. The visit to his son caused C. P. to warm up even more.[22]

This is a great example of repentance that led to social justice and to racial reconciliation.

An unidentified critic of the book and movie affirms several significant outcomes from this experience in race relations.

1. Loving your enemy works: Ann Atwater goes out of her way to help the son of C. P. Ellis who is mentally challenged.
2. The impossible becomes possible: Relationships are necessary to change the world and to change the church. (see Romans 12:10; Ephesians 4:29-32; Colossians 4:12-17)
3. Relationships change hearts: Ann and C.P worked on issues related to integrating the white high school. Working together develops and strengthens relationships.

---

22   Osha Gray Davidson, The Best of Enemies: Race and Redemption in the New South (Chapel Hill, NC: The University of North Carolina Press, 2019).

4. Righteous deeds may lead to suffering: C.P. Ellis did what was right, but he also lost some of his friends. (see Matthew 5:10)

Although all of society should be engaged in efforts to foster racial justice that leads to racial reconciliation, Christians, because they are to emulate Christ in the things they say and do, should be in the forefront of these efforts.

A few weeks ago, I was listening to a sermon by Bishop William Barber in the aftermath of the violent and unnecessary death of George Floyd at the hands of a Minneapolis police officer.

During the sermon, Barber referred to an occasion when he arrived at the airport in a city where he was scheduled to be a guest preacher and didn't see anyone there to meet him. He waited for over an hour, and during that time, he walked by a man who also seemed to be waiting for someone. He walked by the man several times. The next time he walked by, the man asked him, "Are you Rev. Barber?" When he affirmed this, the man told him that he had been given a picture of him that was obviously taken when Barber was somewhat younger. In the picture, Barber had an afro along with his younger features. As the man looked at Barber and looked at the picture, he said:

"You don't look like your picture!"

Christians are to look like Christ. Christians are to emulate Christ. But, when people look at many of us, "We don't look like Christ." When people look at many of us, "We don't look like our picture!"

When we have racist attitudes and engage in racist actions,
"We don't look like Christ."
"We don't look like our picture."

When we fail to respect people of different races and cultures,
"We don't look like Christ."
"We don't look like our picture."

GOD FIRST

When we ignore the plight of the poor and don't do
what we can to help them
"We don't look like Christ."
"We don't look like our picture."

When we do nothing to help make our society better
for everyone,
"We don't look like Christ."
"We don't look like our picture."

When we exclude people of different races and cultures from
our neighborhoods.
"We don't look like Christ."
"We don't look like our picture."

When we exclude people of different races and cultures from
our churches,
"We don't look like Christ."
"We don't look like our picture,"

When we exclude people of different races and cultures from
our schools,
"We don't look like Christ."
"We don't look like our picture."

When we fail to engage in actions to "set the captives free,"
"We don't look like Christ."
"We don't look like our picture."

When we fail to engage in acts of healing wounds
and relationships,

"We don't look like Christ."
"We don't look like our picture."

When we see wrongdoings and say and do nothing to correct them,
"We don't look like Christ."
"We don't look like our picture."

Being a Christian is **more** than attending church. Being a Christian is **more** than reading your Bible. Being a Christian is **more** than being an American.

Being a Christian is to emulate Christ. Being a Christian is to look like Christ. Being a Christian is to follow the example of Christ. Being a Christian is to obey the teachings of Christ. Being a Christian is to live by the Golden Rule. Being a Christian is to live by the Beatitudes. Being a Christian is to live by the Great Commandments to love God and to love others. Being a Christian is to love others as you love yourself.

Being a Christian is to take the gospel to the ends of the earth. Being a Christian is to be inclusive. Being a Christian is to take the Word of God and show the love of God "in Judea, in Samaria, and to the ends of the earth."

The following question should also be in the mind of every person who professes to be a Christian:

"IF YOU WERE ARRESTED FOR BEING A CHRISTIAN, WOULD THERE BE ENOUGH EVIDENCE TO CONVICT YOU?"

Being a Christian is to accept Jesus Christ as the Lord of your life and as the Savior of your soul. Being a Christian is to ask and allow the Holy Spirit to help you live your life according to God's Word.

If you are a Christian, hopefully you're **asking** and **allowing** the Holy Spirit to help you live your life according to God's Word. If you're not doing this, I urge you to do so.

If you are not a Christian, I urge you to **realize** that you need to have a personal relationship with God through Jesus Christ and to **ask** the Holy Spirit to help you to **accept** Jesus Christ as the Lord or your life, as the Savior of your soul, and enable you to have the abundant life that comes from living your life according to God's Word.

CONCLUSION

If more people throughout the country and around the world would live by biblical principles in general and, particularly, by the biblical principles taught by Jesus, we would have a better society and we would have a better world.

It is remarkable that many religions embrace some form of the Ten Commandments and some of them even embrace some from of the Beatitudes. Some people who don't even profess to be religious do likewise. Hopefully, whether you are religious or not, you can see the value in living by these principles.

Since the early 1700s, there have been at least two Great Awakenings that saw a significant increase in the number of people making a commitment to live by God's Word. There were reports of people having life-changing experiences that caused them to become better husbands, better wives, and better people in general.

During these periods, there were changes in attitudes that produced laws and societal changes that moved us more in the direction of our constitutional commitment of "liberty and justice for all."

The year 2020 will be remembered for many things. It will be remembered as the year of the outbreak of the COVID-19 pandemic. It will be remembered that by November more than ten million Americans

GOING TO THE NEXT LEVEL

had contracted the virus and more than 240,000 had died from it because of our overall response as a nation and the insufficient response of our government. It will be remembered as the year when some of our states were not prepared for their primary elections. As a consequence, many Black and other ethnic minority voters were unable to vote because of their unpreparedness. It will be remembered as a year when people of all races, creeds, and colors came together by the thousands in cities across the country to demand that police officers be held accountable for acts of brutality and murder against Black men and women and other people of color.

If we as a nation and individual citizens decide to live by "The Golden Rule." If we decide to live by "The Jesus Rule," we can take a major step toward repentance. We can take a major step toward social justice. We can take a major step toward criminal justice reform and eliminating "the new Jim Crow." We can take a major step toward ending gerrymandering that denies "one man, one vote." We can take a major step toward ending voter suppression and end the "purging" of voter rolls without "due process" that is open and transparent and have the participation, cooperation and approval of both political parties. We can take a major step toward racial reconciliation. We can take a major step toward equal personal, gender, racial, social, educational, and economic opportunity for all Americans.

If we as a nation, as Christians, as people of all faiths, as Democrats, Republicans, and Independents, as Black and White Americans—people of various races, creeds, and colors come together and take these and other necessary steps we can usher in a NEW GREAT AWAKENING that can reverberate throughout the country and around the world.

QUESTIONS FOR REFLECTION & ACTION

After reading this sermon:

1. What acts of repentance will you engage in and when will you do so?
2. What acts of repentance should your relatives and friends engage in?
3. Will you encourage them to do so? If so, when? If not, why not?
4. What acts of repentance should our nation engage in?
5. When and how should we do so?
6. What will you do to foster social justice?
7. What will you do to encourage and help others to foster social justice?
8. What will you do to promote racial reconciliation?
9. What will you do to encourage and help others to do to promote racial reconciliation?
10. When will you start?

GOD FIRST FOR A BETTER LIFE
Matthew 6:33 (NIV)

As we come to the final sermon in this section, let's take a closer look at the title for this book of sermons: GOD FIRST FOR A BETTER LIFE. As we do so, let's take a closer look at Matthew 6:33.

INTRODUCTION

Matthew 6:33 is in the middle of our Lord's "Sermon on the Mount." In chapter five, Jesus focuses on The Beatitudes. In chapter seven, Jesus focuses on judging others, on asking, seeking, and knocking, on the narrow gate, on a tree and its fruit, and on the wise and foolish builders.

In the middle of these two chapters, in chapter six, Jesus focuses on giving to the needy, on prayer, and fasting, on treasurers in heaven and on worry. After instructing His disciples to not worry about what they will eat, drink or wear, in verse 33 Jesus instructs them to

"Seek first His kingdom and His righteousness,
and all these things will be given to you as well." (NIV)

In this remarkable statement by Jesus, we have a principle
and a promise.

The Principle
Seek first the kingdom of God and His righteousness

The kingdom of God refers to the rule of God, the reign of God, and the sovereignty of God. That means wherever God rules and wherever God reigns, that's where God's kingdom exists.

Jesus said that the kingdom of God is in you—believers—because believers have chosen to let God rule and reign in their life. That doesn't mean that believers always do what God wants them to do, but that believers have committed themselves to knowing and doing His will in spite of their weaknesses and shortcomings.

GOD FIRST

Jesus also said that the kingdom of God is among you. This may refer to Jesus as the embodiment of the kingdom of God or to other believers who have committed themselves to knowing and doing God's will.

Jesus also said that the kingdom of God shall come. This probably refers to the fact that God's will is always being done in heaven and that His will is in the process of being done on earth and will someday be done completely.

To seek first the kingdom of God is to want to know and do God's will as our primary objective in life. This objective is reflected in Proverbs 3:5-6:

> *"Trust in the Lord with all thine heart. Lean not to thy own understanding. In all thy ways acknowledge Him, He shall direct thy paths." (KJV)*

This objective is reflected in Paul's statement in Philippians 4:8 where he says:

> *"Finally, brothers, whatever is true, whatever is noble, whatever is lovely, whatever is admirable—if anything is excellent or praiseworthy—think about such things." (NIV)*

Jesus demonstrated the primal importance of knowing and doing God's will in statements like:

> *"My food is to do the will of Him who sent me and to accomplish His work" in John 4:34.*

Jesus' commitment to knowing and doing God's will is reflected in His prayer to God in the garden of Gethsemane when He says:

> *"My Father, if it is possible, may this cup be taken from me. Yet, not as I will, but as You will" (Matthew 26:39, NIV)*

GOING TO THE NEXT LEVEL

Jesus did not just *tell* us to seek first the kingdom of God. He also *demonstrated* the importance of doing so by the things He said and did.

Knowing and doing God's will as our top priority in life is fleshed out in our Lord's command to love God with all of our heart, soul, mind, and strength and to love our neighbor as we love ourselves.

We show that we love our neighbor as we love ourselves by doing all that we can to help others attain the highest quality of life—physically, mentally, spiritually, socially, and economically.

When we really love our neighbor as we do ourselves, we do all that we can to ensure that everyone has access to the best medical care, educational opportunities, employment, and entrepreneurial opportunities. When we really love our neighbor as we do ourselves, we do all that we can to ensure that everyone has an equal opportunity to pursue and achieve "the American dream" in all of its aspects. When we really love our neighbor as we do ourselves, we do all that we can to ensure that everyone has the opportunity to reach his or her potential in every area of life. When we really love our neighbor as we do ourselves, we do all that we can to ensure that everyone has the opportunity to know, to do, and to be and to become all that God created him or her to be.

To love one's neighbor as one loves himself is to want the best for one's neighbor (Shalom) and to be willing to do all that we can do to help others to pursue and achieve the best quality of life.

One of the most unfortunate things in our society is that so many people (especially, successful people) have and express the attitude: **"I've got mine and I'm satisfied!"**

I believe that a truly Christian attitude would be: **"I've got mine and I have an obligation to help others to get theirs!"**

In order for this to happen, there has to be a paradigm shift. In order for this to happen, there has to be a paradigm shift from **"me only"** to **"me and others."** In order for this to happen, there has to be a paradigm shift that embraces the concept of **"Lifting as we climb!"**

235

Most Christians readily affirm that they believe in the Great Commandments (loving God supremely and loving one's neighbor as one loves himself), the Great Commission, the Beatitudes, and the other teachings of Jesus. Some even believe in putting God first in their life. However, the evidence suggests that most professing Christians really don't seek first the kingdom of God and His righteousness.

Most professing Christians probably have a will. And most of them probably leave most (if not all) of their assets to their children and other family members. Some leave some of their assets to their church and to other organizations. However, I believe that few professing Christians leave a substantial amount of their assets to advancing the kingdom of God.

Seeking the kingdom of God includes advancing the kingdom of God.

Advancing the kingdom of God means helping to fulfill the Great Commission of helping people throughout the country and around the world to come to a saving knowledge of God through Jesus Christ, to grow as disciples of Jesus Christ, and to become disciple makers for Jesus Christ in order to glorify God and edify His church.

Seeking the kingdom of God is seeking to know and do God's will. At the heart of God's will is for people around the world to be saved, sanctified, and filled with the Holy Spirit in order for them to know and do and become all that He created them to be. If that is true, it seems to me that professing Christians would want to leave a substantial amount of their assets to ministries that glorify God, that edify His church, and that advance His kingdom.

Question: "What is a substantial amount?"

After the last spouse dies, I believe at least half of one's total assets would be a substantial amount. However, that amount should be determined after much prayerful deliberation asking the Lord for His guidance.

Whatever the amount it could be perpetuated through an endowment for advancing the kingdom of God.

I pray that every committed Christian will seek divine guidance for the things God wants him or her to do to glorify God, to edify His church, and to advance His kingdom while they are alive and after they pass from time into eternity.

According to Revelation 14:13-14— **"Blessed are the dead who die in the Lord… they will rest from their labor, for their deeds will follow them." (NIV)**

One of the great opportunities we have as Christians is that we can be actively involved in glorifying God, in edifying His church, and in advancing His kingdom while we live as well as after we die.

The righteousness of God refers to God's nature. God's nature is reflected in His holiness. The righteousness of God refers to God's perfection. The righteousness of God refers to the fact that God cannot sin or make a mistake.

The righteousness of God refers to the fact that because God is infinitely holy, He is *right* in all that He thinks, says, and does.

When we seek first the kingdom of God, we have our priorities straight. When we have our priorities straight, we seek to have and maintain a right relationship with God. In order to have and maintain a right relationship with God, we allow His nature to "rub off" on us. As God's nature "rubs off" on us, we become more and more like Him. As we become more and more like Him, His righteousness "rubs off" on us.

As God's righteousness "rubs off" on us, we become spiritually righteous. As we become spiritually righteous, this gift of righteousness is reflected in the things we *think*, in the things we *say*, and in the things we *do*.

The Promise
All these things will be added unto you

The principle tells us that instead of worrying about the necessities of life, we should seek first the kingdom of God and His righteousness. This principle ends with a promise: *"All these things will be added unto you."*

In his devotional blog, Shawn Thomas points out that:

"The phrase 'added unto you' is an interesting one. It is actually an old Greek business term that means 'thrown into the bargain.' When sellers in the ancient markets were weighing out their produce, they would toss a little extra in, just to make sure the customer was getting everything they were paying for, and a little more."

Thomas says:

"THAT is what Jesus is saying here: Focus on ME. Focus on My kingdom. Don't serve the gods of material prosperity and success that everyone else is spending their whole lives seeking. Seek HIM instead. And if you will, you may be surprised at how much He 'throws into the bargain'—even material Things—when you commit to HIM first!"[23]

CONCLUSION

If you really want to have a better life, it's imperative that you get and keep your priorities straight. If you really want to get and keep your priorities straight, you must put Christ first.

A song in the New National Baptist Hymnal says this quite well:

---

23   Shawn E Thomas, "'Seeking Him First' (Matthew 6:33 Sermon)," shawnethomas, September 17, 2017, https://shawnethomas. com/2017/09/18/seeking-him-first-matthew-633-sermon/.

GOING TO THE NEXT LEVEL

You may build great cathedrals large or small. You may build skyscrapers grand and tall. You may conquer all the failures of the past. But only what you do for Christ will last.

You may seek earthly power and fame. The world may be impressed by your great name. Soon the glories of this life will all be past. But only what you do for Christ will last.

Tho' your armies may control each hemisphere. And your orbits out in space cause men to cheer. Your scientific knowledge may be vast. But only what you do for Christ will last.

Tho' your songs and prayers are heard and praised by man. They've no meaning unless you have been born again. Sinner, heed these words, don't let this harvest pass. For only what you do for Christ will last.

Remember only what you do for Christ will last. Remember only what you do for Christ will last. Only what you do for Him will be counted at the end. Only what you do for Christ will last.[24]

---

24   The New National Baptist Hymnal

GOD FIRST

CHAPTER SEVEN

OBSERVATIONS FOR REFLECTION & ACTION

"Fixing our Criminal Justice System"
"Fixing our Educational System"
"Fixing our Economic System"
"Fixing our Political System"

FIXING OUR CRIMINAL JUSTICE SYSTEM
Isaiah 1:17 (NIV)

INTRODUCTION

In light of the many social problems and issues plaguing our society, this closing chapter will focus on some personal observations for fixing our criminal justice system, our educational system, our economic system, and our political system.

Obviously, none of these observations will "fix" any of these problems but will simply look at some possible actions that can become part of a more thorough and comprehensive plan.

The observations that will be offered for consideration are informed by Isaiah 1:17 that says: "*Seek justice, encourage the oppressed. Defend the cause of the fatherless, plead the case of the widow." (NIV)*

OBSERVATION

At the heart of creating a just society is the need to begin a serious process for fixing our criminal justice system. Our criminal justice system needs fixing for many reasons. This system needs fixing because it has tended to focus on punishment rather than on rehabilitation and restoration. This system needs fixing because it has imprisoned a disproportionate number of minorities in general and Black Americans in particular. This practice has had a devastating effect on minority families in general and on Black American families in particular. The current system has also given much longer and harsher sentences to minorities and, in some cases, has refused to even prosecute whites for more serious crimes.

According to a report by the Southern Poverty Law Center (SPLC) in November 2019:

Over the past four decades, our country's incarceration rate—the number of prisoners per capita—has more than quadrupled and is now unprecedented in world history.

Today roughly 2.2 million people are behind bars in the United States, an increase of 1.9 million since 1972. We have the world's largest prison population—with one quarter of its prisoners but just 5% of the total population.

And, on any given day, some 7 million people—about one in every 31 people--- are under the supervision of the corrections system, either locked up or on probation or parole.

This vast expanse of the corrections system—which has been called "the New Jim Crow"—is the direct result of a failed, decades-long war on drugs and a "law and order" movement that began amid the urban unrest of the late 1960s—just after the civil rights era.

OBSERVATIONS FOR REFLECTION & ACTION

We're using litigation and advocacy to help end the era of mass incarceration, to root out racial discrimination in the system, and to ensure humane, constitutional standards for prisoners.[25]

The Southern Poverty Law Center is working to radically revise the current system and those groups that advocate for restorative justice are working to replace the system. Work should continue to radially improve the current system as well, to begin replacing it with restorative justice initiatives.

Two very important books dealing with restorative social justice are *The Little Book of Race and Restorative Justice* by Fania Davis and *The Little Book of Restorative Social Justice* by Howard Zehr.

The book by Fania Davis has the subtitle *Black Lives, Healing, and US Social Transformation*. Davis points out that "The United States is a nation born in the blood of the enslavement of Africans and genocide of Native Americans."[26] She contends that

"Americans are socialized to reduce racism to individual expressions of prejudice and overt acts of bigotry. Yet racism in the United States is three-dimensional: structural, institutional, and individual... Structural racism is the normalization and legitimization of white supremacy, enacted from the nation's beginnings, by vast historical, governmental, cultural, economic, educational, institutional, and psychological forces, all working in concert to perpetuate racial inequality."[27]

---

25   (Southern Poverty Law Center, 2019).

26   Fania Davis, The Little Book of Race and Restorative Justice: Black Lives, Healing, and US Social Transformation (New York, NY: Good Books, 2019).

27   Ibid., 32.

Dr. Davis singles out police violence as a major racial and social justice issue. In doing so she notes that:

"Throughout history, police have served as highly visual enforcers of white supremacy who brutally subjugate black communities. We see this in the paddyrollers' capture of escaped slaves, in convict-leasing and debt-slavery- era arrests, in police-assisted lynchings during Reconstruction and the Jim Crow and civil rights period, and, finally, in today's criminalization of blackness and countless killing of black people."[28]

The Vera Institute is one of the strong advocates for police reform. In an article published online (www. vera.org/issues) June 3, 2016, the institute lists Five Reforms Every Police Department Should Make." They suggest the following actions:

(1) **Institute Community Policing:** In order to "optimize positive contact between police officers and community members."

(2) **Demilitarize:** Noting that "In uprisings from Baltimore to Ferguson, a major point of contention was a highly militarized response by police, who greeted nonviolent protesters with military-grade weapons and vehicles."

(3) **Appoint Independent Prosecutors:** To hold officers more accountable for their actions "by ending the grand jury process for officers involved in shootings."

---

28 Ibid., 74.

OBSERVATIONS FOR REFLECTION & ACTION

(4) **Set Up Civilian Complaint Review Boards:** To provide community oversight of police in order to establish greater accountability

(5) **Provide Racial Bias Training:** In order to expose "implicit biases, unconscious prejudices, and stereotypes."

The Role of Police Departments and Police Unions

In order for significant reforms to take place as quickly as possible, police departments and police unions should lead the way by setting the necessary internal standards and procedures and by holding themselves and their fellow officers accountable.

Two police organizations that are taking these initiatives are the United Black Police Officers Association (UBPOA) and the Hispanic Law Enforcement Association (HLEA).

These organizations are not only setting standards for accountability but are also addressing internal systemic structures that make it difficult for ethnic minorities to advance in the ranks of police unions.

In *The Little Book of Restorative Justice*, Howard Zehr contends that "Restorative justice requires, at minimum, that we address the harms and needs of those harmed, holding those causing the harm accountable to 'put right' those harms, and involve both of these parties as well as relevant communities in the process." As he sees it, "Restorative justice is an approach to achieving justice that involves, to the extent possible, those who have a stake in a specific offence or harm to collectively identify and address harms, needs and obligations in order to heal and put things as right as possible."[29]

Sandra Pavelka makes the following observations in an article published in the Fall 2016 issue of the Justice Policy Journal that was addressed to the Center on Juvenile and Criminal Justice.

---

29   Howard Zehr, The Little Book of Restorative Justice: Revised and Updated (Intercourse, PA: Good Books, 2015), 48.

Restorative justice seeks to balance the needs of the victim, offender and community by repairing the harm caused by delinquent acts ... A paradigm shift has occurred in the past two decades as punitive models no longer avail in present-day justice systems. Such a paradigm shift challenges traditional methods that hinder the possibility of solutions that articulate new values and goals in an effort to challenge, rethink, and refocus current systems, policies, and practices.[30]

The current system of criminal justice is woefully inadequate. As a society we can and should and must do better. The restorative justice system has great possibilities and is developing several models in many states. Hopefully, every state will do a serious reevaluation of its criminal justice concepts and practices and make the necessary improvements that will lead to less incarceration and more accountability and more help for offenders to become truly transformed persons as they prepare to reenter society.

Paying a Debt to Society

One of the key concepts of our criminal justice system is that an offender has an obligation to "pay his debt to society." If that is truly the case, why is our society spending more than $30,000 a year to incarcerate offenders?

If offenders were truly paying their debt to society, it should begin with a fixed amount that he or she should pay to each victim and an additional amount that he or she should pay to "society."

In order for this to be possible, offenders would need to be gainfully employed with a significant amount of his or her earnings going to make restitution to his victims as well as to society. In order for that to be

---

30   Sandra Pavelka, "Restorative Justice in the States: An Analysis of Statutory Legislation and Policy," Justice Policy Journal 13, no. 2 (2016), 1-3.

OBSERVATIONS FOR REFLECTION & ACTION

possible, offenders would need the education and the marketable skills that would provide the income needed to sustain a reasonable standard of living while, at the same time, paying his debt to his victims and to society.

Consequently, jail and prison should be limited primarily to violent offenders. By meeting strict requirements, these inmates could earn "release time" to be gainfully employed outside the prison and return at the end of each work day until their sentence is completed.

Those not convicted of violent crimes should spend little or no time in jail or prison in order to **work and pay restitution** to victims as well as to pay their "debt to society."

It must not be overlooked that *the most devastating* and *the most profitable* crimes are **"white collar crimes."** These crimes are committed by corporations that pollute the air and water and do other things that cause sickness, disease, and death to millions of people every year because of their greed and insensitivity. Additionally, the "fine" for violating the rules for these hazards are usually so small that there is no incentive to discontinue them.

In many cases, the financial gain for committing these violations is often in the *BILLIONS whereas the "fine" for doing so is often in the THOUSANDS.* In these situations, "CRIME PAYS!"

As long as they are profitable, these violations will continue.

The only way to stop corporations from continuing to engage in these life destroying violations is to make it unprofitable. Fine the corporations **and** their decision-making executives so it is much more than the **profit** and have substantial **prison sentences** for those convicted executives because of the physical, mental, emotional, environmental, and economic damage that results from their irresponsible actions.

End Mass Incarceration

In an article by the Vera Institute, "Ending Mass Incarceration," it was noted that

GOD FIRST

"Literally millions of men and women are jailed over the course of a year, mostly for crimes related to poverty, mental illness, and addiction, and often because they can't post bail. Even a few days in jail can derail their lives and throw their families into turmoil."[31]

This is a serious indictment of the gross callousness and great insensitivity of our present criminal justice system.

No society should ever be guilty of imprisoning and punishing people who need help because of mental illness, addiction, and because they cannot afford to post bail.

Six out of every ten people in jail are there because they cannot afford to post bail. These people have not been tried. They have not been convicted of a crime but because they cannot afford to post bail, they may be jailed for months—sometimes even years.

This is outrageous. This is barbaric. This is injustice on steroids.

We **must** find a solution to this. We **must** find a reasonable alternative to keeping people in jail simply because they don't have the money to post bail. We **must** correct this gross injustice.

For 40 years, Prison Fellowship has been in the forefront of studying the problems associated with and taking actions to reform our criminal justice system.

In *Outrageous Justice,* Prison Fellowship reports on some of these studies and on some of the actions it has taken and is taking and on some of the actions that other groups are taking to reform and fix our criminal justice system.

---

31   Vera Institute of Justice et al., "Ending Mass Incarceration," Vera Institute of Justice, March 17, 2020, https://www.vera.org/ending-mass-incarceration.

OBSERVATIONS FOR REFLECTION & ACTION

Some of the things that it reports are as follows:
More than 10 million arrests occur in the United States each year.

One in 38 adults are incarcerated, on probation, or on parole.

Approximately 2.2 Americans are incarcerated.

About 4.5 million people are on parole or probation

More than 2 million people have been exonerated since 1989.

Approximately 70 million Americans (one in three adults) have a criminal record.

Black men between the age of 18 to 19 are almost 12 times more likely to become incarcerated than white men. (bold added) (p. 39)

The report also notes that:

States are spending approximately $70 billion on corrections every year. The Bureau of Prisons (the federal prison system) has an annual budget of approximately $7.1 billion and confines 180, 000 people, roughly half of whom are serving sentences for nonviolent offenses .... This equates to our government spending about $39,000 per year to incarcerate each man and woman in prison.[32]

---

32 Craig DeRoche, Heather Rice-Minus, and Jesse Wiese, Outrageous Justice, (Prison Fellowship, 2019), 39-40.

GOD FIRST

These statistics are fueled by the fact that:

The prison population in the United States hovered at or below 200,000 people From the 1920s through the early 1970s. After the 1970s, however, the prison population bloomed.... There were 667 percent more people incarcerated in 2008 than were incarcerated in 1972.... Data shows that there are 1,719 state prisons, 102 federal prisons, and 942 juvenile correctional facilities. **In 1950 there were just 158 prisons (combined, federal, state, and juvenile).**[33]

It does not take a rocket scientist to see that we are **building** an incredible number of prisons, **spending** an incredible sum of money to warehouse thousands of people (**Blacks and Hispanics disproportionally**) who could be part of a more economical and a much more productive accountability system.

According to this Prison Fellowship report, the two primary engines driving this tremendous increase in our prison population are (1) the increase in the length of sentences and (2) the increase in the number of criminal laws.

The report notes that: The War on Drugs and the expansion of mandatory minimum sentencing have played a large role in increasing the average prison term. People released from prison in 2009 served sentences that were on average 36% longer than people released in 1990. In other words, we are punishing people longer today for the same behavior they committed a generation ago.[34]

---

33   Ibid., 40.

34   Ibid., 41.

250

OBSERVATIONS FOR REFLECTION & ACTION

Added to these observations is

"The rapid increase in known wrongful convictions. Since 1989, there have been more than 2,000 exonerations, and in 2017 alone, there were 139. These 2,000 individuals, who were falsely convicted, have wrongfully served more than 19,000 years in prison."[35]

These statistics should make it abundantly clear that our criminal justice system is in need of some significant reforms to eliminate these injustices.

Defund the Police. Really?

One of the most controversial cries during the recent demonstrations in several cities has been "Defund the Police."

The basic concept of this unfortunately ambiguous statement is that police departments spend much of their time doing "social work" that other agencies should be required to do that takes them away from doing all of the "police work" that they are trained to do.

Understood in this context, more funds should be given to other agencies to assist police in dealing with people who give evidence of having a mental illness or that their behavior is influenced by drugs without taking anything from funds that the police need to operate effectively.

Instead of defunding police departments, more funds should be given to police departments for sensitivity training, for skills training in deescalating a serious situation, and to know when to call for assistance from some other agency.

It has been reported that the police chief of the Seattle police department resigned because the department was defunded and officers received a 10% cut in pay.

If that report is true, a tragic mistake was made on the part of those in charge of making such a decision because it had to affect the morale of

---

35   Ibid., 30.

the police department in a time when the city was dealing with a health crisis, an economic crisis, and social unrest.

It would have been wiser to allocate funds to some other agency to do some of the social work that the police had been doing.

Most police officers are professional and want to serve and protect. Consequently, those police officers and unions should not allow their reputation and respect to be tarnished by officers who are insensitive, racist and unprofessional.

Police unions should make it clear that they will not support members who engage in insensitive, racist, and unprofessional actions. Rather than give blanket support to members accused of such actions, unions should advise members to seek legal help.

As I reflect on the need to reform and fix our criminal justice system, the following suggestions are among the basic things that need to be done.

Alternatives to Incarceration

With an overwhelming incarceration population, we need to find viable alternatives to incarceration. Keep in mind that most people are in jail because of drug and mental health issues, and because they cannot afford to post bail. Most people who are in jail need help, not punishment. They need counseling. They need medical treatment and education. They need help getting out of poverty so that they can afford the necessities of life.

Those convicted of a crime should have to pay monetary restitution to the victim, as well as a fine to society that would be significant enough to discourage a repeat offense. Offenders could also be required to do community service.

If the jail and the prison populations were decreased by 5% a year for ten years, we would see a 50% decrease in those populations and we would see a significant increase in our workforce that would add to our tax base. That would be a win-win situation for former prisoners and for society.

OBSERVATIONS FOR REFLECTION & ACTION

Abolish the Alford Plea

One of the most clandestine injustices in our criminal justice system is to allow defendants to utilize what is called the Alford Plea, which allows them to maintain their claim to innocence but permits the court to punish the accused with a prison sentence.

This is ridiculous. Many defendants use this plea rather than run the risk of having a trial and being convicted. The Prison Fellowship report notes that "this has kept many people from having the opportunity to be heard." Consequently, "To protect everyone's right to just process, we must advocate for common-sense code provisions, prosecutorial limits and accountability, and for sufficient resources for public defenders for those who cannot afford their own attorney."[36]

Limit the Authority of Prosecutors

Being a prosecutor is an awesome responsibility. Because so much is expected of prosecutors there is internal or external pressure to get as many convictions as possible.

Sometimes, in order to get a conviction, prosecutors cut corners and don't investigate all of the allegations or present all of the evidence they have. Sometimes, in order to get a conviction, prosecutors pressure the accused to accept a plea bargain in order to avoid a trial that could lead to a conviction.

Because of these and other pressures on prosecutors, some have suggested that it would be better for judges to have a major role in matters regarding plea bargains. Judges are usually not under the same kind of pressure as are prosecutors to obtain a conviction.

Ban the Box

After being released from prison and reentering society, there is the need for employment and housing. Former prisoners have problems at

---

36   Ibid., 31.

this point because on many applications for employment and housing there is a box that asks, 'Have you ever been convicted of a crime?"

When a former inmate answers that question, many employers will not consider him or her for employment. The same or a similar question is often asked on applications for housing. Some renters and some managers of property will not consider renting to those people.

Because of this kind of discrimination that limits employment, housing and other opportunities, many advocates for reform are urging city councils and state legislatures to "Ban the Box," requiring applications to not include a question about previous incarceration.

Things that discriminate against former prisoners and limit their opportunities are seen as a "Second Sentence." These things are unfair and should be eliminated.

Bail Bond Reform

Many people in our society cannot afford to post bail when accused of a crime. Some of these people are unemployed. Some of them cannot find or keep employment because of mental health problems or drug addiction or homelessness. Consequently, they are put in jail without being convicted of any crime simply because they cannot afford to post bail.

This is unconstitutional. This is criminal. This avoids due process. This needs to change.

SIX out of TEN people who are in jail are there because they could not afford to post bail. This is unjust. This is cruel. This is barbaric. This has existed for almost two hundred years in a so-called "civilized society."

What other things can be done?

Since our state governments have failed to correct this injustice for almost two hundred years, churches, community organizations,

OBSERVATIONS FOR REFLECTION & ACTION

and other concerned people should demand that reforms be instituted immediately.

1. People who have never been convicted of a crime and those who are accused first offenders could be released without having to post bond.
2. Churches and other organizations could set up accounts that could advance bail funds to accused people who cannot afford to post bail.
3. Corporations, foundations and people of means could set up accounts to advance funds for posting bail.
4. Concerned groups and individuals should explore and advocate for other ways to keep people from being jailed because they cannot post bail.

The immediate result would be that (1) we would end incarcerating people who have not had due process and who have not been convicted of a crime (2) we could reduce our jail population by 60%.

Consider the Intent

In the book of Exodus, the Israelites were told to consider the intent when considering what should be done to a person who has committed a crime. Was the crime intentional or unintentional? Punishment or restitution or forgiveness was to be administered on the basis of the intent. In considering criminal matters today, this would be a good practice.

Community Policing

In cities that have community policing, the relationship between the community and the police have benefited because these police officers are assigned to a specific community where they get to know and be known by the residents. As a result, a mutual respect and mutual trust has developed. Community policing could benefit many more communities

End Mandatory Minimum Sentencing

In efforts to get tough on crime back in the 80s and 90s, politicians passed laws to mandate mandatory minimum sentencing for drug crimes. Although these laws seemed like a good idea to many at the time, they have resulted in harsher penalties for minor drug offenses, for first-time offenders, and have prohibited judges for using any discretionary judgment.

Identical Sentencing for Crack & for Crack Cocaine

When our governments (state and federal) decided to get tough on crime back in the seventies and eighties, laws were passed that punished crimes involving selling crack and selling crack cocaine one hundred to one (1 to 100).

Meaning, a person would be sentence to ONE YEAR in prison for selling one form of the drug and could be sentenced to ONE HUNDRED YEARS for selling another form of the same drug.

It should be noted that WHITE offenders were primarily the ones selling the cocaine and BLACK offenders were primarily the ones sentenced for selling crack cocaine.

This great DISPARITY is not only UNJUST and UNFAIR but it is also RACIST!

Restore Voting Rights to Former Prisoners

When those convicted of a crime "pay their debt to society" by compensating the victims of their crime, by paying a possible fine, and by completing their sentence, there is no reasonable reason why they should not be able to vote. By not giving former prisoners the right to vote imposes a permanent debt that is unreasonable and unfair.

CONCLUSION

Recently, I heard that a police officer was driving through a community and noticed a woman walking who was on her way to work. According to the report, one morning it happened to be raining, so he asked her could he give her a ride. She accepted the ride and, in conversation with her, the officer learned that this woman walked six miles to and from work each day. He decided to give her a ride on other days, and, when he was not on duty, he asked one of his fellow officers to give her a ride.

According to the report, when information about this woman spread throughout the community, someone gave her a bicycle. According to the report, when the news of her situation reached LET'S MAKE A DEAL host, Steve Harvey, he invited her to his studio and **gave her a check for $5,000 and a brand-new car.**

The officers who were involved in helping this woman should be greatly commended. These officers represent the best police officers who have taken an oath to serve and protect. These are the kind of officers who are needed and appreciated and who should be supported in every community.

As we engage in efforts to fix our criminal justice system, one of the basic things that needs to be done is to create a culture of mutual trust and respect between police officers and communities.

QUESTIONS FOR REFLECTION & ACTION
After reading these observations:

1. What new things did you learn about our criminal justice system?
2. What old ideas about criminal justice do you need to change?
3. What do you plan to do to help others to better understand our criminal justice system?

4. What do you plan to do to help public officials enact rules, regulations, and laws to improve our criminal justice system?
5. What reforms do you believe need to be made to our system of posting bond?
6. What acts do you believe need to be decriminalized?
7. Why do you believe this?
8. Do you believe that our criminal justice system should put more emphasis on rehabilitation and restitution than on punishment?
9. What do you plan to do to encourage your church or your organization to get involved in criminal justice reform?
10. When do you plan to start doing so?

OBSERVATIONS FOR REFLECTION & ACTION

FIXING OUR EDUCATIONAL SYSTEM

Philippians 4:8-9 (NIV)

In verse eight, the Apostle Paul encourages believers to think about things that are true, noble, right, pure, and admirable. In verse nine, the apostle encourages believers to put those things into practice.

As we think about things that are true. noble, right, pure, and admirable, most people would agree that acquiring a good education is noble and admirable.

Most people would agree that to pursue a good education is a noble task. Most people would agree that to acquire a good education is an admirable accomplishment.

The Book of Proverbs places great emphasis on wisdom, knowledge, and understanding. Education is the key to knowledge and understanding and this knowledge and understanding can help one acquires and develop wisdom.

Millions of people in every society are sick, impoverished, and dying because of a lack of knowledge and understanding. Millions of people are unaware of the negative effect that some things have on their physical, mental, and spiritual well-being and on their quality of life. Millions of people are unaware of the negative effect of some things that they eat and drink.

In reality, people really do
PERISH FOR LACK OF KNOWLEDGE

Because knowledge is so important, education (acquiring knowledge) is one of the most important things for people to do. Consequently, this message will focus on improving and fixing our public education system and our college education system. Let's begin by looking at our public education system.

OUR PUBLIC EDUCATION SYSTEM

When I was growing up, the American educational system was ranked as the best in the world. American students scored higher on tests in most fields than did students anywhere else in the world. However, over the past fifty years, our educational system has greatly deteriorated.

In his book, *Foundations of Economic Prosperity*, Daniel Drezner, notes: "Despite the fact that the United States spends more per pupil than any other country in the world, U.S. test scores are consistently mediocre. In 2009, 15-year-olds in the United States ranked 14th out of 34 OEDC economies in reading, 17th in science, and 25th in mathematics."[37] These are disturbing statistics.

According to Drezner, "The OEDC estimates that if the United States could significantly improve its students' test scores in math and science for the current generation, the gain could exceed $100 trillion."[38] This is a staggering projection.

When one reads other data on the cost and quality of our education system the situation looks even more serious.

In order to improve and fix our current educational system, we can begin by removing current barriers to equal educational opportunities.

Change How We Finance Public Education

Removing barriers to equal educational opportunities must start with revising the way we finance our school system. Consequently, viable alternatives to financing school systems primarily through property taxes are absolutely necessary.

---

37   Daniel W. Drezner, Foundations of Economic Prosperity: Course Guidebook (Chantilly, VA: Teaching Co., 2013), 158-159.

38   Ibid., 160.

OBSERVATIONS FOR REFLECTION & ACTION

Some possible considerations are:

(1) Provide supplemental funding for low-income districts from money saved from decreasing our prison population and from other sources

(2) Encourage more affluent school districts to help lower income districts

(3) Encourage corporations and foundations to adopt low-income districts to provide additional funding

(4) Encourage churches and community groups to provide additional resources for low-income districts

(5) Encourage more affluent people (including athletes & entertainers) to donate funds and to raise funds to help low-income districts. The contributions of people like Bill Gates, Michael Jordan, Oprah Winfrey, Rick Warren, Shakira and others have been very helpful. Shakira, the young pop mega-star has paid for the education of thousands of children.

Additional financial resources will make it possible to add other resources and innovations to improve the quality of education for every child in every district. Each district should have a goal to graduate 100% of its students each year.

Prepare all Students to Graduate

Every school district should have a basic goal to prepare all students to qualify to graduate from high school.

Preparing all students to be prepared to graduate from high school must begin in preschool and kindergarten through adequate testing and ongoing observation. This will enable teachers to know the strengths and weaknesses as well as the primary learning style of each student. Weaknesses and other needs should be spotted and addressed early so that they can be eliminated as quickly as possible.

Unfortunately, too many districts ignore these weaknesses and needs in preschool and kindergarten and try to begin to address them much later. By then, it becomes exceedingly difficult and, in some cases, almost impossible.

There is abundant evidence that most learning and growth take place in earlier years. Consequently, we need the most concerned, capable, and creative teachers preparing students to grow, mature, and excel academically in these years.

In order for students to be motivated to learn and grow academically, learning has to be fun and students need to see the benefits and get excited about the benefits of learning at an early age.

In order for all students to be prepared to graduate from high school, there may need to be remedial help for some students. This remedial help should include discovering each student's basic personality type and basic learning style to know and understand "what turns them on" and "what turns them off." When this is discovered, educators will know how to best motivate each student and what incentives need to be employed in order for them to be sufficiently motivated.

Ideally, the value of education should be emphasized in every home. Obviously, this is not the case and there are many reasons why this so.

Unfortunately, some parents don't see the value of education. Some parents have been taught (usually by their parents) that education is not valuable. Some have even been taught to not trust education.

On the other hand, some parents believe in the value of education but don't take the time to instill this value in their children, because they are working two or three jobs just to provide the basic needs for their family.

Many people would be surprised to know how many parents fall into this category. In some of these families, their children have to work after school in order to help the family to keep a roof over their head. That means, these students will have little time or little incentive to do homework in order to keep up in school. That's why it is very important for individuals and organizations to identify and provide help and encouragement for these students and their families.

OBSERVATIONS FOR REFLECTION & ACTION

In order to encourage students, our church in Gary instituted a program where we adopted at least one school each year where criteria were developed by the schools to recognize and honor students who made the most progress from the lowest grades to higher ones and from negative attitudes and behavior to more positive attitudes and behavior. These students were recognized and honored in a general assembly at the end of the school year and given US savings bonds. This recognition was a powerful incentive for some students to continue to improve their grades as well as their attitude and behavior.

School Districts Can Learn from Each Other

School districts can study and learn from each other and can promote innovative programs to enhance the educational experience of their students. School districts that were identified in an article on the internet by Janet Dupre (Jan. 12, 2016) titled "9 innovative schools looking to redefine public education in the U.S." as one's with innovative programs are:

Carpe Diem Schools in Ohio and Indiana

The Alliance School in Milwaukee, Wisconsin

Clintondale High School in Clinton Township, Michigan

STAR School in Flagstaff, Arizona

Brightworks School in San Francisco

Pathways in Technology Early College High School
in Brooklyn, New York

The Primary School in East Palo Alto, California

Quest to Learn in New York

Parkley's Park Elementary School in Park City, Utah[39]

---

39   Katie Dupere, "9 Innovative Schools Looking to Redefine Public
      Education in the U.S.," Mashable, January 12, 2016, https://mashable.
      com/2016/01/12/innovative-public-schools/.

THE NEED FOR A COLLEGE EDUCATION

There was a time when few people in our society had a high school education. There was a time when many people in our society didn't see the need even for a high school education. That time has passed.

Most people in our society today know that having at least a high school education is important and having a college education is even more important. If they did not grow up believe this, by the time they started looking for a job they discovered that they were at a great disadvantage if they were not at least a high school graduate, and, in many cases, at least a college graduate.

Looking at several different metrics, there is evidence that supports the theory of a better overall quality of life for those with an education. Generally, a better education results in: better health care, longer lifespan, more income, the ability to live in a more desirable neighborhood, children getting a better education, more vacations, and a happier life.

Because of these distinct benefits, efforts should be made to make it possible for every high school graduate (especially black and other minority students because they have so many social and economic challenges) to be able to acquire a college education.

As a step to help make up for so many disparities and inequities experienced by African Americans, initiatives should be undertaken to remove all barriers for them to receive a college education. These initiatives should include grants and scholarships for the entire cost of their college matriculation.

Because this nation and its economy was built on the free labor of African-American slaves from 1619 to 1865, their descendants deserve to receive as much education as possible without any economic barriers. The price for doing this could be provided by a combination of investments from the government and corporations, from denominations and other organizations, as well as from individuals.

QUESTIONS FOR REFLECTION & ACTION

After reading these observations:

1. What do you think of the suggestions made to improve our public school system?
2. What suggestions would you include or delete?
3. What do you think of the suggestion to make college more accessible?
4. What are you willing to do to help improve our public school system?
5. What are you willing to do to help make a college education more accessible?

FIXING OUR ECONOMIC SYSTEM
Isaiah 1:17 (NIV)

The two Greek words that form the word economics (*oikos* and *nomos*) literally mean "the rule" or "the law" of the house. Consequently, economic factors limit or afford the opportunity for having an adequate standard of living in every society.

Some believe that because of the free slave labor that was a major factor in creating the enormous wealth of this society and that some form or reparations or restitution would be appropriate for the descendants of those former slaves.

On August 16, 2020, a guest professor on United Shades of America gave a conservative estimate of $19 trillion for enslaved African American labor from 1619 to 1865 at 11 cents per hour at 3 ½ percent interest compounded. No figures were given for inequities since 1865.

Because of the racial and economic disparities and inequities that continue to exist in our society, equal economic opportunities are an essential part of leveling the playing field to social justice that can lead to racial reconciliation.

The Income Gap in our Society is Great and Continues to Expand

The income of Black Americans is two-thirds of that for White Americans, and the unemployment rate for Black American is double that of White Americans. Because of redlining and other factors, Black home ownership is far less than that of Whites. Black people tend to have much more debt and far less in savings than White people.

When it comes to retirement income and net worth, there is a great disparity. When it comes to net worth, there is a great disparity. When it comes to economic factors, White Americans fare much better than Black Americans.

OBSERVATIONS FOR REFLECTION & ACTION

In order to close the income gap, racial, social, political, educational and economic factors are involved and must be addressed. Basic economic factors include employment, homeownership, and entrepreneurship.

Employment

There is no practical reason why every person who wants to be employed cannot find employment that affords him and his family at least a middle-class standard of living in the richest country on the planet.

I'm sure many people would disagree with that statement. But let's be honest—our economic system is not designed and intended to afford the majority of its citizens the opportunity to have at least a middle-class standard of living but to ensure that a few individuals and families can have an exceedingly high income for an exceedingly high standard of living.

If you don't believe this just look at our tax code. Our tax code consists of a million pages of rules and regulations that provide loopholes so that the rich and the super-rich can pay little or no income tax.

These loopholes are provided by our government through laws passed by Congress to allow this to happen. Is it any wonder that these lawmakers receive enormous sums from these individuals and corporations for their campaign and for other things? To make sure that such laws are passed and enacted, these individuals and corporations also pay enormous sums to lobbyists to influence legislation in their favor.

Warren Buffet and other billionaires have affirmed that the system is so skewed and unfair that their secretaries pay more income taxes than they do.

This past week, it was reported that President Donald Trump paid no income tax for ten of the previous fifteen years and that he paid only $750.00 in income tax the year he was elected President as well as the following year.

Is it fair for billionaire individuals and multi-billion-dollar corporations to pay little or no income tax when some citizens pay tens of thousands and some pay hundreds of thousands or even millions of dollars in income tax each year?

This is not fair. This is not fair and it needs to be changed. This is not fair and it needs to changed soon.

This is an appeal for the playing field to be level. This is an appeal for rich and super-rich individuals and corporations to pay their fair share, which should be a minimum percent of their total income.

Home Ownership

Real estate is a valuable asset. Real estate is the most valuable asset that most people have. Therefore, home ownership should be a goal for most people.

The economic gap between whites and minorities (especially African-Americans) can be reduced significantly if more minorities owned property. At the present, 60 to 80% of White American own their home in various parts of the country. But only 40% of Black Americans own their home.

The reasons should be obvious. On the one hand, Black Americans earn only 60% as much as White Americans. Earning 40% less than White Americans means that it is more difficult for Black Americans to save money after paying for their basic needs.

On the other hand, a large percentage of Black Americans don't have the education to secure a higher paying job. Many Black Americans are still discriminated against through redlining when trying to buy a house in certain neighborhoods and through other schemes of discrimination.

For many reasons, it is also more difficult for Black people to get a loan, and when they do get one, many of them have to pay significantly higher interest rates.

OBSERVATIONS FOR REFLECTION & ACTION

These factors are made even worse by the fact that African-Americans are more likely to be arrested, jailed, and imprisoned. There is evidence that Black Americans receive harsher sentences for the same crimes as others. Then, there is the factor that up to 50% of Black men between the ages of 18 and 25 are either in prison, have been to prison, are on their way to prison, or are on parole. Most of them for petty criminal offenses.

One of the unfortunate facts of life is that there are still more Black men in prison than in college. And this will continue being the case until we deal effectively with the inequities of our criminal justice system.

Entrepreneurship

The standard of living gap could be greatly reduced if more Blacks and other ethnic minorities owned and operated their own businesses. Because of unequal educational opportunities, job and housing discrimination and other systemic factors, it is much harder for Black Americans to start, own, and operate their own business. These factors could be greatly eliminated with a significant number of mentors and sponsors.

One of the greatest contributions that the rich and the super-rich can make to our society in general and to help eliminate racial, gender, and income inequalities, is by becoming mentors and sponsors.

One wealthy real estate investor says he has a goal of helping create a million millionaires in ten years through his books and seminars. **If he succeeds, that will add a trillion dollars to our economy.** That would be great. It would also be great if successful people in every business and profession would mentor as many people as they can.

Such a program would be even more effective if those who are mentored would be required to "pay it forward" by making and keeping a commitment to mentor at least one person each year.

In addition to mentoring, more successful individuals and corporations could help our society and our economy by sponsoring new entrepreneurs or by helping them obtain the necessary financing to start a new business.

One of the greatest things that successful people can and should do is to help as many other people as possible to become successful. By doing this they will be living out the implications of Shalom—wanting the best for others at all times and in every way.

Wanting the best for others at all times and in every way is at the heart of "The Golden Rule"—to do the good things for others that people have done for you. It is also at the heart of "The Jesus Rule"—to realize that what you do for others you do for Him. Jesus says, "as you did it to the least of these you did it to Me."

QUESTIONS FOR REFLECTION & ACTION
After reading this observation:

1. What are you willing to do to help create a tax system that levels the field of economic opportunities?
2. What are you willing to do to help remove barriers to economic opportunities?
3. What are you willing to do to help remove barriers to equal employment opportunities?
4. What are you willing to do to help remove barriers to equal housing opportunities?
5. What are you willing to do to encourage individuals and corporations to invest time and other resources in mentoring and in supplying venture capital to entrepreneurs or to helping them acquire the venture capital needed to start new businesses and succeed?

FIXING OUR POLITICAL SYSTEM

"Seek justice. Correct oppression. Defend the fatherless.
Plead for the widow."
Isaiah 1:17

INTRODUCTION

Although our political system has generally served us relatively well for more than two hundred years, it can and should be improved. As we evaluate our political system, some things need to be improved and some things need to be eliminated or fixed.

Anyone who doubts this needs only to look at the fiasco in Florida and in Georgia in 2018 where hundreds of thousands of African Americans were removed from the voting roles without due process. One can look at the gross efforts of voter suppression by closing many polling places in Black neighborhoods, by cutting back on the hours of voting in other places, and of making it harder to vote by requiring voter identifications that are difficult for some people to get.

The right to vote that is guaranteed in our constitution is being eroded by efforts of voter suppression in communities that have a large ethnic minority population in general and a large African-American population in particular.

Coupled with these racial situations there is the corruption of our system by "dark money" being funneled into campaigns illegally.

One of the criticisms of our political system that I have made since I was in high school studying civics is the negative idea and practice of running "against" an opponent rather than running "for" a particular office. Because of this negative emphasis most campaigns focus more on criticizing the opponent than on promoting one's own ideas for improving the community.

I got a taste of this firsthand when I ran for school board in Hammond, Indiana. All of the candidates, except me, focused on negative

GOD FIRST

remarks about the other candidates and little was said by them about what specific things they would do to improve the Hammond school system.

However, I laid out several specific things that I would do to help improve the school system. One thing was to have periodic meetings in various schools to hear ideas and concerns from the parents and other residents of the community. Before long, the other candidates began promoting the ideas that I presented.

Although I did not win a seat on the Hammond school board, several of the ideas that I introduced were co-opted by those who were elected.

Unfortunately, we have woven into the DNA of our political system that candidates run "against" each other rather than "for" the office.

After observing, studying, and participating in our system for many years, I offer the following observations for consideration.

End All Forms of Voter Suppression

The most basic right in a free democratic society is the right to vote. For more than two hundred years, people have championed this right and some have given their lives in order to create and preserve a free democratic society.

I turned 21 in 1959, and I had the opportunity and privilege of voting for the first time in 1960. Since that time, I have voted in every general election and in almost every midterm and special elections in California, Indiana, and Arizona.

I have been a student of political science since high school. As I look at our present system, the following things are among those that need to be addressed.

Increase Vote by Mail and Early Voting Opportunities

This would make it easy for every eligible voter to cast his or her vote without having to go to the polls. Every state should do everything possible to make it easy for citizens to vote and to make sure that their vote is counted.

272

OBSERVATIONS FOR REFLECTION & ACTION

Make Election Day a National Holiday

If every state does not make it possible to vote early or to vote by mail, it would be helpful for elections days, especially for national elections, to be observed as a national holiday. Some people cannot make it to the polls on election day because they work two or three jobs to support their family. If election days were a national holiday, these people would be able to vote without missing work.

Radical Reforms of Campaign Financing

In a free democratic society, every effort should be made to make sure that the playing field is as level as possible. That means: no candidate should be able to "buy" an election because of great personal wealth or because of having many wealthy contributors. I know that this is easier said than done for many reasons. One reason is that every candidate can spend as much personal money as he wants on his or her campaign. Nevertheless, think tanks should be looking at ways to keep this from giving wealthy candidates the financial advantage they currently have.

Reform or End Gerrymandering

Our political system will never work fairly until we either reform or end gerrymandering so that there will be fair representation in all cities, states, and congressional districts. As long as political parties can redraw districts every ten years it will remain unfair. In order to correct iniquities, some states have established non-partisan boards to redraw fairer geographical and population districts after every census. Every state should enact such a system.

Reform or Abolish the Electoral College

Before the year 2000, only two or three candidates had won the popular vote for president of the United States but lost the election because they did not get the majority of votes in the electoral college. This happened again in the 2000 election and in the 2016 election. This should never be allowed to happen again.

The electoral college was set up primarily to increase the political power of Southern slave-holding states that had generally smaller populations than Northern states. As a result, most of our initial presidents were from the South.

In an article from *The New York Times*, by law professor Stephen Vladeck titled "How to fix our election chaos" that appeared in The Week, he notes that:

> The ongoing chaos over the presidential election results is "entirely unnecessary"… The U.S. is unique among advanced nations having each state hold its own election, with its own rules and methods of counting and results coming out in dribs and drabs over days. Those varying rules "led to wild fluctuations as results were updated' last week, with the 'mirage' that President Trump was leading in several states; in reality, votes in Biden's favor had already been cast and were simply waiting to be counted. The delays in counting mail-in ballots and votes from big cities allowed partisan conspiracy theorists to claim 'sinister forces were at work." This system needs to be brought into the 21th. century before the next presidential election.[40]

Many people have defended retaining the electoral college. Regardless of their arguments for doing so, the bottom line is that 538 electors should not be able to override the votes of over 100 million people.

Most people think it would take a constitutional amendment to abolish the electoral college. However, there is a movement currently

---

40 Stephen I. Vladeck, "Elections Don't Have to Be So Chaotic and Excruciating," The New York Times (The New York Times, November 8, 2020), https://www.nytimes.com/2020/11/08/opinion/voting-results-elections.html.

OBSERVATIONS FOR REFLECTION & ACTION

underway where states are mandating that whoever wins the popular vote in their state automatically receives the vote of the electors in the electoral college. Critics say that this would give large states an unfair advantage over smaller states. This concern could be remedied by candidates receiving the percentage of votes from electors that he or she receives of the popular vote. Two states currently do this. Hopefully, the electoral college will be reformed or abolished before the 2024 presidential election.

Elect More Independent Officeholders

According to a recent report, 41% of voters have registered as Independents, 34% as Democrats, and 25 % as Republicans. Although these figures vary from state to state, in order for a candidate to be elected in many places, he or she has to attract a significant number of Independent voters.

Both parties have been guilty of political posturing that has prevented our federal government from working effectively. As a consequence, many bills that are passed in the house never even get a hearing in the senate. To make matters worse, senators still have the privilege and power of exercising the antiquated and undemocratic filibuster.

Looking at these and other realities, if neither the Democrats nor the Republicans had a majority in either chamber, both would have to get a significant number of Independent votes in order for their legislation to pass. Both parties would have to be more open to compromise on policies and pending legislation without compromising their principles.

If neither party had a majority in the house, both parties would have to negotiate with Independents in order to elect the Speaker of the House.

If neither party had a majority in the senate, both parties would have to negotiate with Independents in order to elect the Senate Majority Leader.

Since independent candidates tend to be more moderate, they could have tremendous influence in passing legislation and in keeping both parties from going too far to the right and from going too far to the left.

If neither party had a majority in either chamber, there will be a greater need for the two parties to work together and for them to see the need to be incentivized to work together with independents. Consequently, we need to encourage more people to run for office as Independents, help them get elected, and hold them accountable for helping to avoid extremes and to pass legislation that helps to fix our broken systems, raise the standard of living, and improve the quality of life for all Americans.

Groups like No Labels encourages states to list candidates without listing party affiliations and encourages those elected to work together and to put the public good above party affiliation.

CONCLUSION

As you look at the number of social issues that can and should be addressed it is easy to be somewhat overwhelmed. That is quite understandable. As I reflect on that challenge, let me offer some suggestions for some basic things that each of us can do.

If you are a person of faith make sure to ask continually for Divine Guidance and ask others to join you in doing so.
"Bathe your efforts in prayer!"

Study issues of social justice and other issues and encourage your friends to do likewise

Decide to begin by addressing specific social issues and encourage your friends to do likewise.

Address other issues of concern with public officials and encourage your friends to do likewise.

OBSERVATIONS FOR REFLECTION & ACTION

Commend public officials when they take action, continue to press the issues when they don't take action and encourage others to do likewise.

When the desired legislation is passed, be aware of and take a stand against efforts to circumvent its enforcement and encourage friends to do likewise

Join and/or support groups with the same concerns and encourage friends to do likewise
Stay informed. Stay concerned. Stay involved.

P.U.S.H
Persist Until Something Happens (the results you desire) and Encourage Friends to do Likewise
In order to strengthen your efforts, make sure to get as many people involved as possible

QUESTIONS FOR REFLECTION & ACTION
After reading these observations:

1. What are you willing to do to improve our criminal justice system?
2. What are you willing to do to improve our educational system?
3. What are you willing to do to improve our economic system?
4. What are you willing to do to improve our political system?

GOD FIRST

PERSONAL COMMITMENT

TODAY, I accept Jesus Christ as my Lord and Savior. With the help of the Holy Spirit, I will become a disciple of Jesus Christ and a disciple maker for Jesus Christ. In order to glorify God, edify His Church, and advance His Kingdom, I will encourage others to do likewise.

With the help of the Holy Spirit, I will do what the Lord leads me to do to live out the implications of The Golden Rule and The Jesus Rule and encourage others to do likewise.

In the Name of Jesus. AMEN!

_____

Name

_____

Date

If you would like to share this decision with me,
you may send it to colvin25@netzero.com

OBSERVATIONS FOR REFLECTION & ACTION

PERSONAL RE-COMMITMENT

TODAY, I re-commit myself to the lordship of Jesus Christ. With the help of the Holy Spirit, I re-commit myself to be being a disciple of Jesus Christ and a disciple maker for Jesus Christ. In order to glorify God, edify His Church, and advance His Kingdom, I will encourage others to do likewise

With the help of the Holy Spirit, I will do what the Lord leads me to do to live out the implications of The Golden Rule and The Jesus Rule and encourage others to do likewise.

In the Name of Jesus. AMEN!

_____

Name

_____

Date

If you would like to share this decision with me,
you may send it to colvin25@netzero.com.

OBSERVATION

If you have been helped by any portion of this book, you may wish to tell others about it. As you think of the people you know and love, you may wish to give them a copy—especially for special occasions like:

Anniversary
Birthday
Christmas
Easter
Graduation
Mother's Day
Father's Day
Other

Royalties from the book will be used to expand our mission to glorify God, to edify His Church, and to advance His Kingdom throughout the country and around the world.

OBSERVATIONS FOR REFLECTION & ACTION

CONTACT INFORMATION
Colvin Blanford Ministries
Dr. Colvin Blanford, President
24525 S. Rocky Brook Drive
Sun Lakes, Arizona 85248-6254

SEMINARS INCLUDE
Christian Parenting
Evangelism & Discipleship
How to Be Debt Free
Marriage Enrichment
Prayer & Spiritual Warfare
Principles & Practice of Preaching
Richer Relationships

RECOMMENDED RESOURCES
God is Able by John Maxwell
God's Generals by Roberts Liardon
Houses of Prayer Everywhere by Alvin J. Vander Griend
Intercessory Prayer by Shelly Hollins
The 8 Laws of Leadership by Elmer Towns
The Master Plan of Evangelism by Robert Coleman
The Master's Plan for Making Disciples by Win & Charles Arn
The Prayer Saturated Church by Cheryl Sacks
The Purpose Driven Church by Rick Warren
The Purpose Driven Life by Rick Warren
The Strategy of Satan by Warren Wiersbe
101 Ways to Your Wife's Heart by Rosie Allen
101 Ways to Your Husband's Heart by Nick Allen
The Eight Systems of the Church by Nelson Searcy
The Renegade Pastor by Nelson Searcy
Subscribe to "Growth Points" by Gary McIntosh

ABOUT THE AUTHOR

Colvin Blanford, Rel.D.

DR. COLVIN BLANFORD earned his doctorate at the Southern California School of Theology at Claremont and organized churches in San Francisco, Chicago, Gary, Indiana, and Mesa, Arizona. He served as director of Black Church Studies and associate professor of ministry at Northern Seminary teaching in the areas of Black church studies, preaching and social ethics. He has also ministered on missions to Liberia, Malawi, South Africa, Swaziland, and Nigeria.

Pastor Blanford and his wife, Margaret, have been happily married for 57 years and have two sons and several grand and great-grandchildren.

REFERENCES

Alexander, Michelle. *The New Jim Crow: Mass Incarceration in the Age of Colorblindness*. New York: New Press, 2020.

Bennett, Lerone. *Pioneers in Protest*. Baltimore: Penguin Books Inc, 1969.

Davidson, Osha Gray. *The Best of Enemies: Race and Redemption in the New South*. Chapel Hill, NC: The University of North Carolina Press, 2019.

Davis, Fania. *The Little Book of Race and Restorative Justice: Black Lives, Healing, and US Social Transformation*. New York, NY: Good Books, 2019.

DeRoche, Craig, Heather Rice-Minus, and Jesse Wiese. *Outrageous Justice*. Prison Fellowship, 2019.

Drezner, Daniel W. *Foundations of Economic Prosperity: Course Guidebook*. Chantilly, VA: Teaching Co., 2013.

Dupere, Katie. "9 Innovative Schools Looking to Redefine Public Education in the U.S." Mashable, January 12, 2016. https://mashable.com/2016/01/12/innovative-public-schools/.

Evans, Tony. *Let's Get to Know Each Other*. Nashville: T. Nelson, 1995.

Justice, Vera Institute of, Ruth Delaney, Elizabeth Kai Hinton, Insha RahmanAlison Shih, Jaeok Kim, Jullian Harris-Calvin, Andrew Taylor, et al. "Ending Mass Incarceration." Vera Institute of Justice, March 17, 2020. https://www.vera.org/ending-mass-incarceration.

The New National Baptist Hymnal. Nashville, TN: National Baptist Pub. Board, 1981.

Parks, Catherine. *Real; The Surprising Secret to Deeper Relationships*. The Good Book Company, 2018.

Pavelka, Sandra. "Restorative Justice in the States: An Analysis of Statutory Legislation and Policy." *Justice Policy Journal* 13, no. 2 (2016).

Publication. Southern Poverty Law Center, 2019.

SPROUL, R. C. *What Is Repentance?* Ligonier Ministries, 2019.

Stamps, Donald C., and J. Wesley Adams. *The Full Life Study Bible: New International Version*. Grand Rapids, MI: Zondervan Pub. House, 1992.

Stevenson, Bryan. *Just Mercy: a Story of Justice and Redemption*. Melbourne: Scribe, 2020.

Thomas, Shawn E. "'Seeking Him First' (Matthew 6:33 Sermon)." shawnethomas, September 17, 2017. https://shawnethomas.com/2017/09/18/seeking-him-first-matthew-633-sermon/.

Vladeck, Stephen I. "Elections Don't Have to Be So Chaotic and Excruciating." The New York Times. The New York Times, November 8, 2020. https://www.nytimes.com/2020/11/08/opinion/voting-results-elections.html.

Zehr, Howard. *The Little Book of Restorative Justice: Revised and Updated*. Intercourse, PA: Good Books, 2015.

CPSIA information can be obtained
at www.ICGtesting.com
Printed in the USA
LVHW042002220323
742311LV00005B/369